MS-DOS
Training Guide

Clifford Mould

Pitman

PITMAN PUBLISHING
128 Long Acre, London, WC2E 9AN

A Division of Longman Group UK Limited

© Clifford Mould 1990

First published in Great Britain 1990

British Library Cataloguing in Publication Data
Mould, Clifford
    Training guides : M. S – D. O. S.
    1. Microcomputer systems. Operating systems : MS – DOS
    I. Title
    005.4469

    ISBN 0–273–03172–4

Printed and bound in Great Britain

Typeset by 𝔽 Tek Art Ltd, Addiscombe, Croydon, Surrey

Contents

Introduction

The purpose of this Training Guide is to help the user to become familiar with the world's most commonly used disk operating system for personal computers, MS–DOS or DOS for short. Although this operating system will finally be superseded by others such as OS/2, the number of computers in which it is installed is now so large that the majority of personal computer users are likely to meet it for many years.

While it is possible to isolate users from MS–DOS, it has been found that familiarity with the basic DOS commands gives people the confidence to deal effectively with the day-to-day running of their computers, and even more importantly, to sort out some of the problems associated with file and disk management. It is especially true that those who are taking courses in computer studies at GCSE, A or BTEC level will gain valuable insights into the workings of computers by having a thorough familiarisation with the operating system.

After practising the activities in the Guide, you should be able to use the basic internal DOS commands to format disks, perform routine backups and even create some simple but effective DOS programs.

Note to computer managers or tutors

One of the difficulties of producing a simple step-wise practical guide to MS–DOS is the variety both of different hardware configurations and also of the versions of DOS software. It is not possible to make assumptions that the user will be working on a stand-alone computer with a hard disk and one floppy drive, or that they will be using a particular version of DOS.

In order to try to accommodate the problems associated with different drive configurations, it is proposed that a practice disk is set up and accessed as drive B. This is based on the earlier convention that with a dual floppy drive machine you install the systems or program disks in drive A and the data disks in drive B.

In the case of machines with one floppy drive only, which is called A by default, the disk can be inserted and the drive letter changed quite simply by typing B: `ENTER` at the A> prompt. Hard disk users can set up a practice subdirectory on the hard disk and then use the **subst** command to substitute the name B for the subdirectory path, e.g. **subst b: c:\practice**.

Where a machine boots from the server and has no floppy drive at all, such as an RM Nimbus TN workstation, the network manager can set up a RAM drive and assign the letter B to it: e.g. **assign b=c**.

Setting up the practice disk

To make sense of the exercises, you will need a set of dummy files on which to practise various operations including copying, renaming and deleting disk files. To minimise the risk associated with operations involving disk writes, it is essential that a practice disk is copied for your use. The following dummy files will need to be created on the master disk:

memo1.txt	admin.com	cmjoe.mem	memo2.txt
setup.bat	cmsue.mem	memo3.txt	menu.bat
cmliz.mem	btree.com	admin.dat	salary.90
sales.dat	equip.90	account.exe	nominal.dat
salary.feb	budget.wks	account.ovl	cash.wks
spell.ovl	chq.wks	help.doc	basic.com

In order to illustrate file security, and save unnecessary work restoring files lost by accidental deletion, the files should all be set to read only using the command **attrib +r *.***

Creating the files: There are a number of ways of doing this; the following is a simple suggestion:

1 Create the following batch file:

```
copy con f.bat ENTER
echo practice file >%1
Ctrl-Z ENTER
```

2 Then type:

```
f memo1.txt ENTER
```

and a file called memo1.txt will be created containing the two words 'practice file'. If you have any difficulty with this then you probably need to brush up on your DOS!

The only problem is that all the files will be the same length in bytes which will look a little unusual when you list them with **dir**. It would be a good idea to include several other files, or even copy some real files into some of the file names listed above. The file readme.txt needs to contain some text and should be longer than 24 lines so that it scrolls up the screen.

Setting the path to DOS external commands

It would be better not to include external commands such as **format** on the practice disk, because students will be taught that commands can be issued from any subdirectory provided that a **path** has previously been set.

To make certain that you can access external commands satisfactorily these should all be located in a subdirectory called \bin, or \DOS or whatever, and the command **set path c:\;\bin**; or whatever is appropriate to the machine should be executed from within the autoexec.bat file on boot up.

If you are not sufficiently *au fait* with setting up machines, study Section B, Task 12 where the concept of the **path** is first dealt with, followed by Section D of the guide where configuring a machine is explained.

Background to MS-DOS

MS-DOS stands for **M**icro**S**oft **D**isk **O**perating **S**ystem. Microsoft is the large American software company that produced these programs. In this guide the system will mostly be referred to simply as 'DOS'.

The operating system of a typical IBM or IBM compatible personal computer comes in two distinct parts:

1 the BIOS which is supplied as part of the hardware by the computer manufacturer. BIOS (**B**asic **I**nput **O**utput **S**ystem)

2 the Disk Operating System, which is supplied either by the manufacturer, or often by the dealer who sells the computer. DOS can be located on any of the following media:
- a floppy disk
- a hard disk or 'fixed disk drive'
- a network server
- a ROM cartridge or tape cartridge (unusual).

DOS is loaded into the **R**andom **A**ccess **M**emory (RAM) by programs residing in ROM.

The BIOS controls the most fundamental or low-level operations of the computer's hardware. Programs in ROM enable the computer to boot up when you first switch on the power. First the memory and peripherals (e.g. keyboard, printer) are checked, then a search is made for the Disk Operating System, starting with the floppy disk drive, then the hard disk or perhaps a network server.

The BIOS is rather like the subconscious part of your brain that controls heart-rate, reflex activities etc. You cannot communicate directly with the BIOS to override its automatic control of the hardware function any more than you can directly interfere with signals controlling your heart!

DOS itself provides the primary interface between you and the computer so that you can issue commands to set up the working environment, load and run applications programs as well as managing files, disk organisation and other housekeeping tasks.

The DOS interface is called the Command Processor. This means that you have to type in a command according to the exact syntax of the DOS command language. If the Command Processor recognises it as a correct command it will be executed. If not, probably because you have mis-typed the command, an error message such as 'Bad command or filename' will appear.

This is one of the things about DOS that gives it a bad name. Syntax and its dreaded family of error messages is not held to be user-friendly.

Nevertheless, this guide will help you to learn at least the basic commands. Using the simple batch file techniques outlined later in the book, you will be able to create a more user-friendly menu interface for yourself and other users.

The ultimate in user-friendly interfaces is provided by the environment known as **W**indows, **I**cons, **M**ouse and **P**oint (WIMP). This environment was first introduced on the APPLE Macintosh computer, and has been adapted for the IBM PC family. However, people who know their basic DOS will find that they can do things a lot more quickly by pressing a few buttons than by using a mouse.

DOS and UNIX

If you come across the UNIX multi-user operating system you will find that everything that you have learned in DOS about environment variables, pipelines, redirection, filters and replaceable parameters will stand you in good stead.

In UNIX the set of commands available to you is very much richer and some useful applications can be developed using the operating system programming language. Such programs are called **shell scripts** and they form an important and dynamic part of the continually evolving UNIX environment.

Files and disks

When you use a program such as a word processor or a database, the data that you work on is stored in the computer's internal memory (RAM). When the computer is switched off, the contents of the RAM memory is lost, so programs and data need a permanent home.

All programs and data are stored on disks as **files** which are identified by their respective filenames, e.g.

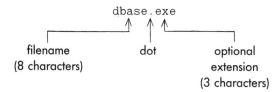

dbase.exe

filename (8 characters)   dot   optional extension (3 characters)

The first part of the filename may have up to eight characters including the letters A–Z, the numbers 0–9, and certain other characters **except for** " : / ? *
Examples of valid filenames:

Accounts.dat   config.sys   memo12   1.bat   temp.$$$

(Note that DOS does not distinguish between upper case (CAPITALS) and lower case letters: lower case is used throughout this text.)

The following filenames would not be allowed:

accounts.data   extension too long
accounting.1   filename too long
memo/jdh   rogue character /

The optional extension is a useful way of telling what sort of file you are dealing with. Here are some typical conventions:

com	command	program or command file
exe	executable	program
bat	batch	program made up of DOS commands
sys	system	contains data about system configuration
bas	basic	program written in BASIC
prg	program	program written in dBASE
pas	pascal	program written in PASCAL
ovl	overlay	subprograms
doc	document	text file
dat	data	data file
ndx	index	dBASE index
wks	worksheet	spreadsheet data

MS-DOS variants

PC-DOS (**P**ersonal **C**omputer **D**isk **O**perating **S**ystem) is the version of MS-DOS sold by IBM for use on its own range of personal computers.

MS-DOS comes in a number of versions. The earliest you are likely to meet is DOS v2.0, while the latest version is DOS v4.1a (1989). If the computer is booted up with one version of DOS and then a DOS external command from a different version is invoked, errors may occur, so take care. You can easily tell which version is resident in memory by typing ver ENTER.

Throughout this book, ENTER means press the ENTER or RETURN key.

Windows is a Microsoft processing environment which utilises pictures called icons. A mouse device is used to point to options symbolised by the icons or to open pop-up windows. DOS v4 can use some of these features.

MS-DOS commands

When the computer boots up, the program **command.com** is loaded into memory (RAM). This program includes a number of basic commands such as **dir** and **copy**. They will remain in memory as long as the computer is switched on. These commands are called **internal** commands.

Other DOS commands and utilities are provided on floppy disk or will have been copied to the hard disk. These are called external commands and will only run if the disk or directory that contains them is on-line.

Using your keyboard with MS-DOS

ENTER

Always press the **enter** key ENTER when you have finished typing a command. This is used as a signal to DOS to begin processing the command.

Computer keys and typewriter keys

Computers never use the lower-case 'l' as a *one*, '1'. Be careful also to differentiate between a *zero* '0' and the upper-case letter 'O'.

There are additional keys on the computer that have special functions, both to DOS and to other programs you will use.

Cursor control keys

The spacebar moves the cursor along to the right, one character at a time.

The backspace ← key deletes characters as it moves the cursor to the left.

The direction, or **arrow** keys ↓ ↑ ← → are not normally used in DOS command processing.

Control key combinations

The control key Ctrl, located to the left of the keyboard, enables the transmission of special codes to the command processor. You must hold down the control key while you press another key, as you do when using the shift key. Control key combinations are written **Ctrl-S**, or sometimes **^S**.

Ctrl-S stops the screen display from scrolling;

Ctrl-C cancels the processing of a command;

Ctrl-Z acts as the end of file marker.

Ctrl-Alt-Del Pressing all these three keys simultaneously causes the computer to restart. If you do this while a program is running you could lose valuable data.

The function keys

In DOS the most recently typed command remains in a storage area called the template. Using the current template together with the Insert ENTER and Delete Del keys, you can:

repeat a command without retyping it;
edit or amend incorrect commands;
alter commands that are similar to one another.

How the editing keys work

Key	Explanation
F1	copies a single character from the template to the command line
F2 *c*	copies all characters up to the character specified
F3	copies all characters to the command line
Del	skips a character in the template
F4 *c*	skips the characters up to the character specified

Esc	aborts the current command leaving the previous command unchanged in the template
Ins	enables characters to be inserted until **Ins** is pressed again
F5	copies the current command line into the template without executing the command
F6	saves having to type **Ctrl-Z** which is the end of file marker

Practical exercises using MS-DOS ━━━━━

The best way to become a competent MS-DOS user is to practise using the commands. As when practising the piano or learning to play a new game, you can easily make mistakes to begin with.

Such mistakes cannot harm the computer itself, but can cause you to lose data held in files, some of which may not belong to you. It is best to do your work on a floppy disk which contains only practice files so that if you make a serious mistake all will not be lost! Your computer manager should provide one for you to use. Instructions about how to do this are in the section on p. v.

Starting a practice session

Follow the steps . . .

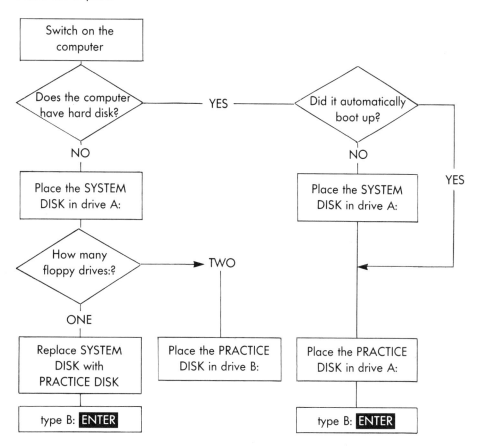

Whatever disk drive configuration you have, the computer should now be displaying a system prompt B>, or B:\>, depending on how your computer has been set up.

The system prompt tells you which the active or logged-in drive is. A single floppy drive can be referred to as A: or B:. If there are two floppy drives, the left or upper one will be referred to as A: and the other one as B:. The hard disk drive is normally referred to as C:.

Networked machines

If you are using a computer which boots up from a local area network, you will need to consult your tutor or network manager before starting work on the activities.

Section A: Simple internal commands ━━━

Task 1   Getting started

Objectives

To reset the system date and time.
To find out which version of DOS is resident in memory.
To practise logging on to different drives.

Instructions

If you followed the steps in **Starting a practice session** on page x, you should be logged on to drive B: with the practice disk correctly inserted in the disk-drive. If you have not done this turn back and follow the steps carefully.

The system clock

All IBM PC compatible computers have an internal clock. In many cases it will be powered by a battery so that it will continue to work even when the computer is not switched on. If there is no clock, a default time and date will appear on the screen every time the computer is booted up.

The screen display will look similar to this:

```
Phoenix 80286 ROM BIOS Version 3.07
Copyright © 1986 Phoenix Technologies Ltd
All rights reserved

640K Base Memory, 00384K Extended

Current date is Mon 1-01-1980 ←──────────── [This is the default date]

Enter new date (dd-mm-yy): 10-01-90 ENTER  ←──── [Enter the correct date]

Current time is 18:43:18.68 ←──────────── [This is the default time]

Enter new time: 10:30 ENTER  ←──────────── [Enter the correct time]
```

Note: the date may appear on screen as mm-dd-yy.

Every time you create or amend a file, DOS will record the time and date of this activity in the disk directory. If you do not check that the date and time are correct, incorrect and confusing information may be recorded.

Activity 1.1   Resetting the date:

Type the command:

date `ENTER`   (**Note:** `ENTER` means press **enter** or **return**)

The computer responds:

```
Current date is Tue 06-03-1990
Enter new date (dd-mm-yy):          ENTER
```
↑_____|

DOS is waiting for you to enter the date in the format day-month-year, separated by two dashes

e.g. 24-05-90 if the current date is the twenty-fourth of May 1990

Note: your computer may have been set up so that dates are displayed in American format: mm-dd-yy (month-day-year)

Activity 1.2   Resetting the time:

Type the command:

time `ENTER`

The computer responds:

```
Current time is 12:00:12.34
Enter new time:        ENTER
```
           ↑_____|

DOS is waiting for you to enter the time in 24 hour clock format: hours:minutes:seconds.fraction of a second e.g. 10:30 (you need not worry about seconds)

If the error messages

```
                Invalid time
```
        or
```
                Invalid date
```

appear, it is probably because you have made a mistake in the format. Perhaps you forgot the dash (minus sign) separating the parts of the date, or you did not insert a colon between the hours and minutes when setting the time.

Activity 1.3   How up-to-date is DOS on your machine?

Check which version of DOS has been loaded into memory by typing:

`ver` ENTER

the computer should respond with a similar message to this:

`IBM Personal Computer DOS Version 3.30`

Activity 1.4   Changing the current drive

If you have a hard disk, try logging on to it by typing:

`C:` ENTER

The prompt should change to C> or C:\>, depending on how it has been set up.

If you have another floppy disk-drive, or no hard disk try changing to the 'A' drive:

`A:` ENTER

The prompt should change to A> or A:\>

Troubleshooting

Even if you have not had any problems with changing drives, the examples below are bound to happen sooner or later. You will learn a lot by deliberately trying to make a mistake which causes one of the error messages below.

Problem 1

```
B:\>A;
Bad command or filename
```

This is the most common error message of all and will appear when you type A; (semicolon) instead of A: (colon)

DOS is very particular about certain things such as a colon after the drive letter, but it does not mind whether you type commands in CAPITAL LETTERS or in lower case letters.

Problem 2

```
B:\>c:
Invalid drive specification
```

This message appears when you do not have a drive 'C'. Try changing to a drive called Q just to see what happens!

Problem 3

```
B:\>A:
Not ready error reading drive A
Abort, Retry, Fail?
```

This means that you have tried to log on to an empty floppy disk drive. You could try putting a disk into the drive and pressing R to retry, or you could press F for fail, in which case the prompt:

```
Current drive is no longer valid>
```

will eventually appear. In this case type B: **ENTER** to get back to where you started from!

Problem 4

```
B:\>a:
```

```
Sector not found error reading drive A
Abort, Retry, Fail?
```

This means that you have loaded a disk that DOS cannot recognise. The error may be caused by:

1 the disk is new or has not been formatted
2 the disk belongs to a non-IBM compatible computer
3 the disk has become corrupted

Press **F** for fail and then at the prompt

```
Current drive is no longer valid>
```
type: B: **ENTER**

Key words	Date
	Time
	Ver

Task 2   **The Directory command**

Objectives   To list files in the current directory.

Instructions   **Dir** is probably the most widely used DOS command. Whether you are using a floppy disk or a hard disk, at some stage you need to know what files are on the disk. If you are trying to find a particular file you will need some way of listing the contents of a disk or directory.

Activity 2.1   The **dir** command

Log into the practice floppy disk in drive B:

    b: `ENTER`

Then type the command:

    dir `ENTER`

A list of files will scroll up the screen. You will probably miss the first few if there are many files in the current directory.
   The **dir** command shows on the screen useful information about the files. **Dir** also returns a count of the number of files present in the directory and tells you how much space (measured in bytes, or characters) is left on the disk. The last lines of the directory listing should look something like this:

```
CMLIZ     MEM      78    12-31-89    7:12p
EQUIP     90       16    12-31-89    7:08p
SALARY    90      268    12-31-89    7:15p
SALARY    FEB      16    12-31-89    7:09p
README    TXT     142    12-31-89    7:15p
ADMIN     BAT      94    12-31-89    7:12p
CASH      CHQ     110    12-31-89    7:13p
        34 File(s) 214162 bytes free
```

Space for 214,162 characters is left on the disk

5

Adding 'switches' to the **dir** command

When the list of files is too long to be displayed on the screen you can stop it from scrolling by adding the '/p' (pause) switch to the command:

`dir/p` ENTER

This tells **dir** to display a page at a time and then pause while you read the information.

Now look more closely at the information that is displayed:

```
B:\>dir \ p
```

Volume in drive B is DOS_EXAMPLE   ⟵——— This is what the disk is called.
Directory of B:\ ⟵——————— This indicates that you are in the root directory

F	BAT	24	12-31-89	6:54p	
ACCOUNTS	DAT	16	12-31-89	6:55p	these are the filenames
MEMO3	TXT	16	12-31-89	7:05p	
BTREE	COM	16	12-31-89	7:05p	their size in bytes
MEMO1	TXT	16	12-31-89	7:04p	
MEMO2	TXT	16	12-31-89	7:04p	the date and time they
BASIC	COM	16	12-31-89	7:05p	were last updated
ACCOUNT	EXE	16	12-31-89	7:06p	
BUDGET	WKS	16	12-31-89	7:06p	
CASH	WKS	16	12-31-89	7:06p	
CHQ	WKS	126	12-31-89	7:13p	
AUTOEXEC	BAT	16	12-31-89	7:06p	

Strike a key when ready . . ._

Press any key when you are ready to see more filenames.
Alternatively, a number of files can be displayed using the 'wide format' switch: **/w**

Type `dir/w` ENTER

The display will look similar to this:

```
Volume in drive B is DOS_EXAMPLE
Directory of B:\
```

F	BAT	ACCOUNTS	DAT	MEMO3	TXT	ADMIN	BAT
BTREE	COM	MEMO1	TXT	MEMO2	TXT	SALES89	DAT
BASIC	COM	ACCOUNT	EXE	BUDGET	WKS	CASH	WKS
AUTOEXEC	BAT	ADMIN	EXE	ADMIN	COM	SETUP	BAT
ADMIN	DAT	NOMINAL	DAT	ACCOUNT	OVL	HELP	DOC
CMSUE	MEM	CMLIZ	MEM	EQUIP	90	SALARY	90
README	TXT						

        34 File(s) 234168 bytes free

Note: although less information is shown, more files can be displayed in the wide format listing.

| **Activity 2.3** | Displaying a particular file — command 'arguments' |

You may want information about a particular file that you believe to be on the disk. Rather than having to scan through several screenfuls of other files, you could include the filename as the 'argument' to the command. An argument is data on which the command can operate. There is always a space between the command and its argument, e.g.

```
Command     space    Argument
   |___        |       ___|
      \        \      /
       V        V    V
       DIR      ACCOUNT.DAT
```

Now type: DIR AUTOEXEC.BAT `ENTER`

If the file is present on the disk you should get a display like this:

```
B:\>DIR AUTOEXEC.BAT

Volume in drive B is DOS_EXAMPLE
Directory of B:\

AUTOEXEC BAT            16  12-31-89  7:06p
           1 File(s)    234162 bytes free
```

Troubleshooting

Read this section even if everything has run smoothly. Try making deliberate mistakes to see if you can get the error messages described below.

Problem 1

```
B:\>DIR AUTOEXEC.BAT
No File
```

This means that you have mis-spelled the filename, or that a file of that name does not exist.

If there is not a file on your disk called autoexec.bat, try substituting a filename that you have discovered earlier.

Problem 2

```
B:\>dirautoexec.bat
Bad command or filename
```

This has appeared because you did not leave a space between the command **dir** and its argument **autoexec.bat**

| **Key word** | **Dir** |

Task 3

'Wild' characters * and ?

Objective

To find particular files by using * and ? in the command argument.

Instructions

In the previous activity, you tried looking for a particular file. If you did not type the name correctly the 'No file' error message was returned. In real life situations you will often be unable to remember the exact name of a file. For instance, you will know that there are a number of files on the practice disk beginning with the word 'memo', and you want to select the most recent one.

Activity 3.1

Listing all the 'memo' files

All files beginning with 'memo' and continuing with any other combination of characters can be displayed by substituting the wild character * (referred to as 'star' or 'asterisk') for the unknown characters:

    DIR MEMO*.* `ENTER`

(This is usually spoken aloud as 'D I R space MEMO star dot star'.) The following will now be displayed onscreen.

```
Volume in drive B is DOS_EXAMPLE
Directory of B:\

MEMO3  TXT  3216   01-03-90   7:05p
MEMO1  TXT   156   12-31-89   3:04p
MEMO2  TXT   216   12-31-89   3:14p
        3 File(s)    323584 bytes free
```

Now look for all files beginning with the letter A

    dir A*.* `ENTER` (Say to yourself 'D I R space A star dot star')

Continue to practise by looking for files beginning with other single letters or groups of letters, for instance, look for files starting with C, B or SAL then make up examples of your own.
If you have any problems it will probably be because you have left out the space between DIR and the argument. Get used to saying to yourself 'D I R space B star dot star', or whatever the argument is.

Activity 3.2

Listing files with the same extension (file type)

It is often very useful to be able to list all the files which have the same extension:

    dir *.com `ENTER`   ('D I R space star dot COM')

The following will then be displayed on screen.

```
Volume in drive B is DOS_EXAMPLE
Directory of B:\

BTREE   COM  3416    12-12-87     8:05a
BASIC   COM  9806    05-23-88    10:05a
ADMIN   COM  1650    12-08-89     7:06p
          3 File(s)    323584 bytes free
```

The three files listed are all of **command** file type

Now find all the files ending in .exe by typing:

dir *.exe **ENTER**

Then list all text files by typing the command:
'D I R space star dot TXT'

Other groups of files to look for might end in:
.wks   .dat   .bat   .doc

Note: Make sure you do not leave out the space after DIR. There are **never** any spaces inside a filename.
Also, make sure you do not leave out the **dot**. DOS itself does not display the dot in directory listings which is rather confusing.

Activity 3.3

The ? wild character

The question mark — **?** is another 'wild' character which can be used to substitute a single character in a particular position in the file name.

Type: dir/w *.?at **ENTER**

You should see a display similar to this:

```
Volume in drive B is DOS_EXAMPLE
Directory of B: \

F       BAT    ACCOUNTS  DAT    AUTOEXEC  BAT    SETUP    BAT
MENU    BAT    ADMIN     DAT    NOMINAL   DAT    ADMIN    BAT
     8 File(s)    323584 bytes free
```

Note that DOS has substituted the letters B and D in place of the question mark immediately after the dot in the command argument.

Key word   Dir

Task 4   **Subdirectories and pathnames**

Objectives

To understand the directory tree structure.
To create new subdirectories.
To move about the tree structure.

Instructions

You will recall that when you first used the **dir** command a long list of files scrolled up the screen.

If your computer has a hard disk, hundreds of files could be stored on it causing the directory to become very full. Coping with such a long and unstructured directory list would be difficult even allowing for use of the wild characters '*' and '?'.

To get around this problem DOS uses a tree-structured system of subdirectories. Imagine a manual filing system in a small estate agent's office. There could be three filing cabinets. The first might contain the details of properties for sale. The other two could hold files on vendors and purchasers respectively. Suppose each cabinet had three drawers: the property cabinet would have one drawer for flats, another for terraced houses and the third drawer would contain details of detached houses. The vendors' cabinet might be arranged by clients' names alphabetically, the top drawer for clients A–H, middle for I–Q and the lower drawer for R–Z. The purchasers' cabinet might also be arranged in three price bands according to what the client is prepared to pay.

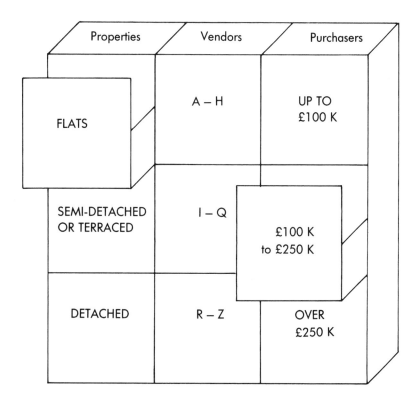

Inside the drawers there could be further subdivisions into folders and finally the files themselves.

This arrangement could be shown as a tree structure like this:

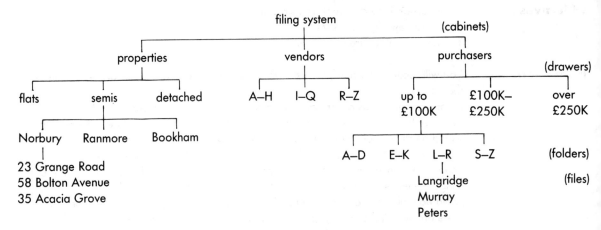

Using the DOS subdirectory system you can set up a structure similar to this. Files that belonged together would be kept in separate subdirectories so that they could be easily located.

<table>
<tr><td>Paths</td><td>

The start of the tree system is called the ROOT directory which is symbolised by the reverse oblique character '\' or back-slash. In the tree diagram above, the route from the root directory to the individual file 'Murray' is called the **path**. We show the path from root to Murray like this:

</td></tr>
</table>

Paths

The start of the tree system is called the ROOT directory which is symbolised by the reverse oblique character '\' or back-slash. In the tree diagram above, the route from the root directory to the individual file 'Murray' is called the **path**. We show the path from root to Murray like this:

    \purchasers\up to £100K\L–R\Murray

Activity 4.1   Which directory am I in now?

To display the current directory, type:

CD `ENTER`

The display should be as below.

    B:\

The '\' tells you that you are in the root directory of drive B:

Your computer may have been set up to display the current directory within the prompt itself. If so your prompt will look like this:

    B:\>

otherwise it will probably look like this:

    B>

Activity 4.2   Setting the prompt to display the current directory

First reset the prompt to its default by typing:

    `prompt` **ENTER**

To display the current directory and path, type:

    `prompt $P$G` **ENTER**

$p displays the path, $g displays the greater than sign.

Activity 4.3   Creating a new directory structure

You will now create a directory structure based on the properties branch of the estate agent example above.
To make a new directory use the command **mkdir**, or **md** for short. The argument to the command is the name of the directory you want to make.

    `md properties` **ENTER**

Note: You will need a space between the command **md** and the argument PROPERTIES.
The floppy drive light will flash to show you that DOS is writing data to the drive. No message will appear unless there is a problem.
To check that the new directory is there, use **dir** as follows:

`dir prop*` **ENTER**

```
Volume in drive B is DOS_EXAMPLE
Directory of B:\

PROPERTI      <DIR>     10-02-90  10:09a
  1 File(s)     322560 bytes free
```

Note that DOS restricts directory names to eight characters, (*see* p. ix).
You could rename the directory PROPERTY by typing:

    `md property` **ENTER**
    `dir prop*` **ENTER**

The following would be the result on screen:

```
Volume in drive B is DOS_EXAMPLE
Directory of B:\

PROPERTI    <DIR>  10-02-90  10:09a
PROPERTY    <DIR>  10-02-90  10:15a
    2 File(s)    321536 bytes free
```

To get rid of the directory PROPERTI, use the command **rmdir**, or **rd**, which stands for **R**emove **D**irectory.

      rd properti `ENTER`

You will look at the command **rd** in more depth later on.

Activity 4.4

Creating subdirectories further down the tree

In order to create a subdirectory below PROPERTY you must first log into the directory PROPERTY.
To find out which directory is your current directory type:

      cd `ENTER`

(You should still be in the root directory.)
Now type:

      cd property `ENTER`

If you have set the prompt to show the path it should be displaying:

      B:\ PROPERTY>

You can always display the current directory by typing

      cd `ENTER`

Note: **CD** means **C**urrent **D**irectory when it is typed without any argument.
'cd space argument' means **C**hange **D**irectory to the one specified in the argument.
You should now be in the subdirectory PROPERTY. Create these subdirectories lower down, as shown on p. 13.

      MD FLATS `ENTER`
      MD SEMIS `ENTER`
      MD DETACHED `ENTER`

Check that all has gone to plan by typing:

      DIR `ENTER`

Your screen should look like this:

```
B:\PROPERTY\>DIR

Volume in drive B is DOS_EXAMPLE
Directory of B:\PROPERTY

                <DIR>  10-02-90    10:15a
.   .           <DIR>  10-02-90    10:15a
FLATS           <DIR>  10-02-90    10:57a
SEMIS           <DIR>  10-02-90    10:57a
DETACHED        <DIR>  10-02-90    10:57a
    5 File(s)    317440 bytes free
```

The entire contents of the directory PROPERTY now consists of other directories, the three new ones you just made with **md**, and two strange ones, 'DOT' and 'DOT DOT'. These are links from the parent directory which is **property**, and child directories. You can ignore them for all practical purposes.

Activity 4.5   Creating a lower level of subdirectories

Look at the tree diagram on p. 12. There is a further sub-division of the structure below SEMIS. You must make the directories which will be used to store files on semi-detached houses in the areas Norbury, Ranmore and Bookham.
To make the new subdirectories under SEMIS you must first **change directory** to SEMIS.

     cd semis `ENTER`

The prompt should be showing the path:

     B:\PROPERTY\SEMIS>

To make the three directories, Norbury, Ranmore and Bookham, type **md** space then the name of the directory and press enter.

Check your work by typing: dir `ENTER`

You should have the following screen display:

```
B:\PROPERTY\SEMIS>DIR

Volume in drive B is DOS_EXAMPLE
Directory of B:\PROPERTY\SEMIS

.               <DIR>  10-02-90    10:57a
.   .           <DIR>  10-02-90    10:57a
NORBURY         <DIR>  10-02-90    11:16a
RANMORE         <DIR>  10-02-90    11:16a
BOOKHAM         <DIR>  10-02-90    11:16a
    5 File(s)    313344 bytes free
```

Finally, change into one of the subdirectories:

`cd ranmore` ENTER

The prompt will be quite long now, because of the lengthy path from the root directory down to RANMORE.

Activity 4.6   Moving back up the path towards the root directory

Your current path should be:

`\PROPERTY\SEMIS\RANMORE`

If you wanted to get back into the directory above, i.e. SEMIS, you could do this quite simply by typing:

`cd ..` ENTER

This means 'change directory to the parent above'

If you type `cd ..` again you will be returned to the directory PROPERTY. Repeat the command to get back to the root directory.
So far you have been moving about one step at a time. To go straight from the root directory to the BOOKHAM directory you will have to give the complete path from root to BOOKHAM as the argument which follows **cd**:

`CD \PROPERTY\SEMIS\BOOKHAM` ENTER

To jump directly to the root directory without stepping back through each parent directory you should type:

`cd \` ENTER

Note: \ is the symbol for root.

Activity 4.7   Moving about a directory structure

If you are not already in the root directory type: cd \ ENTER and then change to the subdirectory FLATS ...

If you were given the error message: **Invalid directory** it was because you typed **cd flats** when you were not in the parent directory of FLATS, i.e. in PROPERTY. There is no directory called FLATS immediately below root. If you have not managed to get into FLATS yet type:

```
cd \ property \ flats  ENTER
```

Now change directly to DETACHED, this time do not forget to include the complete path as the argument following **cd** (space).

From DETACHED, go directly to NORBURY. When you have done that correctly you should return to root.

Activity 4.8   Further practice

Set up the PURCHASERS branch of the tree on p. 12. Use the name lowprice instead of 'up to £100K', and midprice and topprice for the other branches immediately below purchasers. You may make mistakes at first; the only real way to learn is to work it out for yourself.

Key words   **cd (change directory)**
md (make directory)

Task 5   **Looking at files**

Objective   To display the contents of a file.

Instructions   So far you have been looking at the information displayed about files by the command **dir**. You will now learn how to see what is actually inside the file.

Activity 5.1   Displaying a file with the command **type**

Make sure that your practice disk is in drive B, then change to the root directory, if you are not there already:

     `cd \`   ENTER

Use the **dir** command to see if there is a file called readme.txt:

     `dir read*` ENTER

The command **type** will display the contents of file given as its argument:

     `type readme.txt` ENTER

Activity 5.2   Suspending the display with Ctrl–S

Files longer than 24 lines will scroll up the screen, and the top of the file will vanish. You can suspend scrolling by holding down the Ctrl key and pressing S. Pressing any key will reactivate the display.
Locate the Ctrl and S keys before you enter the command **type readme.txt** ENTER and press Ctrl–S as quickly as you can after pressing the ENTER key. You can press any key, such as the space bar, to continue the display.

Activity 5.3   Investigate files on other drives

The general form of the command to do this is   `type filename.ext`

Space ─┘   └─ The full name
                      of the file

e.g. `type memo2.doc`

However, only text files, or data files in standard **ASCII** character format can be displayed using type. If you try to read a program file which consists of binary machine code instructions, the screen will be filled with garbage, the machine will beep at you and you may find the keyboard locks up. In other words, the computer will 'hang up'.

Note: the files on the practice disk are only dummy files so you should not come to any harm with them.
   As a general rule you can usually display files with the following extensions:

 .doc .txt .asc .bat .msg .prg .pas .c

Files with no extensions will usually **type**, and those with README in the name are an invitation to do so!
Files with endings .com and .exe are *not* **type**-able.
Now change to another drive and look for suitable files to **type**.

Key words   **Type**
Ctrl–S i.e. hold down **Ctrl** and press **S**

Task 6

Using the commands

Objective

To use the commands learned so far to investigate the files and directories on a disk.

Instructions

If your computer has a hard disk you will need to change to drive C:

    C: **ENTER**

If you are on a dual floppy drive make sure that there is a disk in drive A:

    A: **ENTER**

If you are on a network consult the network manager before continuing.

Activity 6.1

Looking for directories

You should be in the root directory of whichever drive you are logged on to. If you simply type **dir** **ENTER**, all the directories and files will be listed mixed up together. To display the directories only, type:

    dir *. **ENTER** (DIR star dot ENTER)

```
Volume in drive C is DISK1_VOL1
Directory of C: \

SYS      <DIR>        11-20-89    12:26p
DOS      <DIR>        11-20-89    12:38p
WORD     <DIR>        11-20-89     5:59p
CM       <DIR>        11-23-89     6:31p
S                 26   4-10-89     9:36p
LOTUS    <DIR>        11-20-89     6:02p
ORDERS   <DIR>        11-20-89     6:06p
MEMO     <DIR>        11-23-89    10:03a
MIS      <DIR>        11-23-89     6:35p
ITOS     <DIR>        11-23-89     6:27p
TEXT     <DIR>        11-28-89    11:30a
DB3      <DIR>        12-13-89    12:24p
QC2      <DIR>        12-13-89     4:10p
W        <DIR>        12-18-89     8:29p
FILES    <DIR>        12-31-89     6:06p
BACKUP   <DIR>        12-31-89     6:10p
D                549  12-31-89     6:17p
      17 File(s)    23146496 bytes free
```

You can easily see which the directories are because of the <**DIR**> in the second column of the display. You will see that there are several files in the listing with no extensions, called S and D. If you have any such files with no extensions you could try using the type command on one of them straight away, e.g.

```
type filename
```

Now change to one of the directories on your disk.

```
cd directory name
```

Look for files ending in .doc or .txt or with no extension at all by typing:

```
dir *.doc
```

or

```
dir *.txt
```

etc.

Note the exact name of hopeful looking files and then read them using the **type** command.
Change to another directory and see what you can find there. You could draw up a tree-map of the directory structure starting from the root directory.
Do not attempt to use **type** on files ending .com or .exe.

Key words	Dir
	Type

Section B: File housekeeping ▰▰▰▰▰

This chapter will show you how to maintain files and directories. One of the most important regular tasks which should become a habit is making copies, called 'backups', of working files. Sooner or later every computer user wishes they had taken the trouble to do this!

Task 7

Copying files between directories

Objective

To copy files between devices and directories.

Instructions

Files can be copied between the directories on a single drive, or from one drive to another. They can be copied one at a time or as a group. Copying from device to device might involve transfers between the hard disk and a floppy disk, or from an input device such as the keyboard to a disk file, or even from a disk file to a printer or other output device.

All these activities can be performed by using the **copy** command which becomes memory resident whenever the computer is booted up and DOS is loaded.

Activity 7.1

Copying files from one directory to another on a single disk.

Make sure the practice disk is in drive B and that you are in the root directory.

Copy the file MEMO1.TXT to the subdirectory \PROPERTY which you made in Activity 4.2, by typing the command:

```
COPY  MEMO1.TXT  \PROPERTY ENTER
```

If all goes correctly DOS will respond with the message:

```
1 File(s) copies
```

Notice that there are two arguments to the command **copy** in the example above. As usual, each argument is separated by a space. If an error message appeared the chances are that you left out a space.

To check that there is a copy of memo.txt in the directory \PROPERTY you should type:

```
dir \property ENTER
```

The computer responds:

```
Volume in drive B is DOS_EXAMPLE
Directory of B:\ PROPERTY

.                  <DIR>        10-02-90    10:15a
. .                <DIR>        10-02-90    10:15a
FLATS              <DIR>        10-02-90    10:57a
SEMIS              <DIR>        10-02-90    10:57a
DETACHED           <DIR>        10-02-90    10:57a
MEMO1     TXT             16    12-31-89     7:04p    ←————— There it is!
   6 File(s)    312320 bytes free
```

The general syntax of the **copy** command is like this:

If the optional second argument is not specified, than DOS assumes the destination to be the current directory.
Try another one:

```
copy menu.bat \property  ENTER
```

Then type DIR \ PROPERTY again to see if it is there.

Activity 7.2

Using wild characters to copy a group of files

You can use the 'wild' characters '*' and '?' just as you did with the **dir** command to identify a group of files. Type the commands:

```
cd \  ENTER
```

```
dir /w memo*.*  ENTER
```

The computer responds with:

```
Volume in drive B is DOS_EXAMPLE
Directory of B:\

MEMO3     TXT    MEMO1     TXT    MEMO2     TXT
   3 File(s)    312320 bytes free
```

You can copy the three memo files as a group by typing:

```
copy memo*.* \property  ENTER
```

23

This time DOS should respond with a list of the files and the message:

```
3 File(s) copied
```

Now copy all the files with the extension .dat to the directory below PROPERTY called FLATS.

Try to work this out for yourself: after the command **copy** you will need a space, then the source argument 'star dot DAT' then another space followed by the destination directory path.

You should get a list of all the files ending in .dat and the usual message: *n* file(s) copied, where '*n*' should be a number greater than 1.

If you have problems it is probably because you typed:

```
copy * .dat \ flats or flats ENTER
```

DOS returned the message 1 file(s) copied because you have not properly specified the destination argument. DOS has taken you literally and has copied all three files into a single file called FLATS instead of into the subdirectory \ PROPERTY \ FLATS

You should have typed:

```
copy *.dat  \property\ flats ENTER
```

Activity 7.3   Copying files into one destination file

Try copying all the files beginning with the letter A to the subdirectory SEMIS leaving out the full path to see what happens ...

```
copy A*.* semis ENTER
```

DOS will list all files beginning A but will tell you that only one file has been copied. Check what has happened by typing:

```
dir semis ENTER
```

Notice that SEMIS appears as a file, not a directory. You have discovered this by mistake, but it is a useful function of **copy**. Suppose a number of people were working on a project together. Each could create a document called doc1, doc2, doc3 etc. Then the command **copy doc*.* report** could copy all the doc files into one file called report. This process is known as **concatenation**. (Catenary is another word for chain.)

Activity 7.4   Using only the source file argument

Change to the subdirectory RANMORE.
Work this out for yourself if possible, referring to p.14 only if necessary.
Now copy all the files ending .txt from the root directory by typing:

```
copy \*.txt ENTER
```

Because no destination argument was given DOS assumes you want to copy all files in the root ending in .txt to the current directory.
Check that this has happened by typing `dir` ENTER
Now change your current directory to BOOKHAM and copy *all* the files in PROPERTY directory to the current directory. Try it yourself first; if it does not work think about what you did. Remember that DOS does exactly what you tell it according to its rules of syntax.

Key words   Copy

Task 8

Copying files between devices

Objective

To learn how to copy data between differing peripheral devices.

Instructions

The peripheral devices of a personal computer system enable the input, output and permanent storage of data which is to be processed in the central processing unit (CPU). The keyboard and VDU together are considered by DOS to be an Input/Output (I/O) device called the **console**, or **con**.

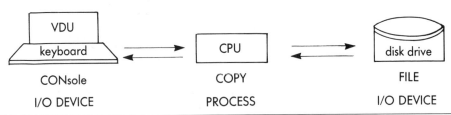

| CONsole | COPY | FILE |
| I/O DEVICE | PROCESS | I/O DEVICE |

Activity 8.1

Copying from the keyboard to a disk file

Make sure that you are in the root directory of drive B:

You can copy a stream of characters from the console to a file by the command **copy con file** substituting a destination filename or path for the word file. For example:

```
copy con test  ENTER
```

The cursor will move down to the next line. Type in this short paragraph:

```
This is a file called TEST created by me.  ENTER
ENTER
I copied a stream of characters from the keyboard  ENTER
which is a standard input device,  ENTER
called the CONSOLE  ENTER
into this file by using the command  ENTER
ENTER
COPY CON TEST  ENTER
Ctrl-Z  ENTER          Hold down the  Ctrl  key and press Z
1 File(s) copied   Confirmation that the file is written
```

Now display the contents of the file using the **type** command:
type test ENTER

Ctrl-Z is called the **end-of-file** marker (EOF). Pressing the **F6** key is an alternative method of sending this control character to signal the end of the file.

This is a simple way of creating a short text file. If you make a mistake, and you notice it before you get to the end of the line, you can make a correction by using the backspace delete key. You cannot move the cursor up the screen in an attempt to edit a previous line because you are not in a screen editor. You are simply copying a stream of characters from one device to another.

Activity 8.2

Creating your own simple text file

Make a text file using the **copy** command. Call the file by your name (up to 8 letters long) followed by the extension .msg which is the standard abbreviation for a message file, e.g.

```
copy con jane.msg
```

End the file with `Ctrl-Z` `ENTER` (or `F6`) and then use the **type** command to display it, e.g. `type jane.msg` `ENTER`

Activity 8.3

Copying to a standard output device.

You will need a printer connected to your computer to be able to do this activity. DOS refers to the printer by the device name PRN or LPT1 if it is connected via the parallel port at the back of the computer. If the commands below do not work, ask your computer manager for help.

Copy the text of the file readme.txt to the printer:

```
copy  readme.text  prn ENTER
```

If you have not got a printer, you can copy the file to the screen part of the console (**con** is also an output device).

```
copy  readme.text  con ENTER
```

The effect is similar to the **type** command. As you learn more about DOS you will discover that there is often more than one way to do something.

Activity 8.4

Printing an envelope

Feed an envelope into the printer, lining it up as if to print an address. Then type:

```
        copy  con  prn ENTER
Mary Richardson ENTER
Computer Manager ENTER
C.B. Enterprises Ltd ENTER
Barnwell Manor ENTER
London NE 12 ENTER
Ctrl-Z ENTER
```

When the cursor moves down to the next line, type the name and address, but **do not** press the `ENTER` key at the end of each line.

When you have finished, type the end-of-file marker, `Ctrl-Z` `ENTER` and the address will be printed on the envelope.

Activity 8.5	Setting up a mailing list

In Activity 8.3 you typed in an address and it appeared on the envelope. Imagine that now, a few weeks later you want to address another letter to the same correspondent. Rather than typing it in all over again, this time type the address into a temporary file called ADDRESS.TMP, copy it to the printer and then add it, or rather concatenate it, to the main address file called ADDRESS.DAT.

Step 1

```
copy con address.tmp ENTER
```

Type the address, with a carriage return ENTER either side of the end-of-file marker (Ctrl-Z).

Step 2

Now set up the printer with a new envelope, and type the command:

```
copy address.tmp prn ENTER
```

Step 3

Finally, copy the temporary address file to the main address file:

```
copy address.dat + address.tmp address.dat ENTER
```

Now repeat steps 1 and 3 several times, adding a new address each time. Display the contents of the file address.dat by entering the command:

```
TYPE ADDRESS.DAT ENTER
```

and you will see your mailing list. This data file can be used by the mail-merge function of a word-processing package such as WordStar.

You have to be quite careful when adding files together and returning the sum to one of the source files. If you get the files in the wrong order the rather frightening error message 'Content of destination lost before copy' will appear.

Note: When adding files together, the safest procedure is:

```
copy file1 + file2 + file3 + file(n)    new file
        └─── source files ───────┘       └─destination file
```

If the destination is also a source file, then the order must be: COPY file1+file2+file3 file1
i.e., the file to be updated must always be the first one in the source list.

Copying from one disk to another will be covered later on in the book when you have made a new disk using the **format** command (see p.53).

Key words	Copy con
	Ctrl-Z
	Copy readme.txt prn

Task 9   Deleting files from a disk

Objective   To identify and delete files.

Instructions   At times you will need to remove unwanted files from a disk that has become cluttered, as disks that become too full can cause serious problems. In task 7 you will have copied a number of files into the subdirectory. \ PROPERTY. Now you can purge the directory using the **del** (delete) command.

Before continuing with the activities, check that the practice disk is in drive B: and that the current directory is B: \ (root).

Activity 9.1	Deleting a single file
Step 1	Change to the directory where the file is located:

cd \ property **ENTER**

| **Step 2** | Use **dir** to display the list of files: |

dir /p **ENTER**

| **Step 3** | Pick the file memo1 to delete. You will need to supply the full name of the file as the argument to the command **del**, so type: |

del memo1.txt **ENTER**

Type **dir** again; memo1.txt should have gone. Choose another file from the list and delete it. The general form of the command is:

del filename **ENTER**

Activity 2	Deleting a group of files using 'wild' characters

You want to delete all the MEMO files. You could do this by typing del m*.*, but be careful, there may be other files beginning with the letter M which you want to keep. Follow the steps:

| **Step 1** | Check that you are in the correct subdirectory by typing cd **ENTER** |
| **Step 2** | Check that the wild card combination you will use specifies the exact set of files you want to delete: |

dir me*.* **ENTER**

```
Volume in drive B is DOS_EXAMPLE
Directory of B: \ PROPERTY
MEMO1    TXT  16   12-31-89    7:04p
MEMO3    TXT  16   12-31-89    7:05p
MEMO2    TXT  16   12-31-89    7:04p
MENU     BAT  16   12-31-89    7:07p
4 File(s)    304128 bytes free
```

You should not use the argument me*.* in this case, because the file menu.bat will be deleted.

Type the command:

dir memo*.* `ENTER`

Step 3   If the MEMO files are the only ones to be listed, then you can safely use the argument memo*.* with the **del** command:

dir memo*.* `ENTER`

Use **dir** again to see which files remain in the directory. See if there are any groups of files that can be specified using *, then follow the three steps until no files are left. Notice that the subdirectories are not touched by **del**.

Activity 9.3   Attempting to delete 'read only' files

Now move to the root directory of the practice disk and try to delete all the files ending in .dat using the three steps rule:

Step 1   cd \ `ENTER`

Step 2   dir*.dat `ENTER`

Step 3   del*.dat `ENTER`

If the disk has been set up correctly you should see the error message:

Access denied

because all the files have been set to 'read only' status. This means that you can read the contents of files but not amend, update or delete them. A whole disk can be protected physically against accidental erasure by having the write protect slot covered, or in the case of the smaller 3½ inch disks, the switch can be set to read only. This disk cannot then be used as a work disk since nothing new can be written to it. Such a disk is regarded as a master disk or reference disk. These physical protection methods are similar to the way you protect audio-cassettes by removing the plastic lugs at the back of the tape cartridge.

Activity 9.4	Deleting the entire contents of a directory in one operation
Step 1	Always change to the directory where files to be deleted are located:

```
cd \property\semis ENTER
```

Step 2	Use **dir** to check exactly which files are there:

```
dir /p ENTER
```

Step 3	If you are certain that you wish to delete all the files, type:

```
del *.* ENTER
```

DOS responds with the message:

```
Are you sure, (Y/N)?
```

This gives you a chance to change your mind; if you are in any doubt at all, press N **ENTER** and type **dir** once more and have another careful look at the directory listing. Only if you are quite certain should you press Y **ENTER**. Check what has happened by typing

```
dir ENTER
```

Undeleting files   You cannot undelete files unless you have a special utility program purchased separately from DOS. When you delete a file using the **del** command, DOS removes the filename from the directory and releases the space it occupied for other files that may be written to the disk at a later time.

Provided that no new file is written to the disk immediately after a file has been deleted, it should be possible to recover the deleted file. If you delete an important file by mistake, you should either:

1 Recover it from the backup, or

2 Remove the disk from the drive if the lost file was on a floppy disk. If the file was on the hard disk switch off the computer and, if necessary, disable it by removing the power cable or disconnecting the keyboard to prevent another user from inadvertently creating a new file over the deleted one, or

3 Obtain a utility package, such as Norton Utilities, and hope it will work. When you resume your work with the computer, back up important files before you do anything else!

The best ways to avoid losing files by careless deletion are:

1 Always change to the home directory where the file(s) are to be deleted. Never try to delete files on a different drive or directory.

2 Always use **dir** with the same argument you intend to use with **del**. If the argument works with **dir** it will work with **del**.

3 Protect files using the **attrib** command, see Section C, p.61.

4 Protect master disks physically by covering the write protect slot.

Key words   **Del**

Task 10

Removing directories

Objective

To locate and remove subdirectories.

Instructions

Occasionally a subdirectory will become redundant and you will want to remove it to tidy up the disk. The command **rmdir** or **rd** short for **R**emove **D**irectory, can be used. To remove a subdirectory you must be in the parent directory:

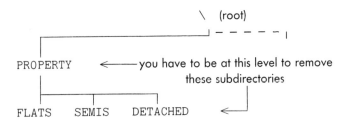

Activity 10.1

Some revision

Make sure you are in the root directory of drive B.

Before continuing ensure that some files in the directory are in DETACHED by copying all the .bat files from the root directory to DETACHED.

Now move to the parent directory of the one you want to remove:

cd \ property **ENTER**

and remove the directory:

rd detached **ENTER**

DOS will return the error message:

Invalid path, not directory or directory not empty

This shows you that DOS will not let you remove a directory and its contents wholesale. The directory must be empty of files before you can proceed, so go ahead and delete all the files from the directory DETACHED. Do not forget the three steps:

Step 1

Move to the directory where files are to be deleted.

Step 2

Use the **dir** command to check that the files can be safely deleted.

Step 3

Delete files using the command **del** *.* **ENTER**

Activity 10.2   Removing the directory

Move back to the parent directory:

    cd .. `ENTER`

Remember that 'cd dot dot' moves you back one step up the tree.

    rd detached `ENTER`

No message is returned if the command operates successfully. To be on the safe side type **dir** to see that DETACHED has gone at last.

Activity 10.3   Removing the other subdirectories under PROPERTY

You should be able to do this without any further **help except** to remind you that:

1 You must be in the parent directory
2 The directory you are trying to remove **must be empty.**

Activity 10.4   Remove the directory PROPERTY

What is the parent directory of PROPERTY? Check that PROPERTY is empty before dropping down to the parent level and removing it. If necessary refer to the answers on p.120.

Key words   **rd (remove directory)**

Task 11　　Renaming files

Objective

To rename files using the **copy** and **ren** commands.

Instructions

When you used the **copy** command in task 7 and 8, you were copying files from one device or directory by creating duplicates of the source files on the destination device. It is also possible, using **copy**, to create a duplicate file with a different name from the source file. This can be useful, for instance where you wish to create a standard document which will require different versions from time to time.

Activity 11.1

Set up a practice directory

Make sure that you are in the root directory of the practice disk in drive B.

Make a directory called TASK11

Change directory to TASK11

Copy all files from the root directory

(If you cannot remember how to do these jobs, see pp.13, 23.)

Check that there is a file called SALARY.FEB in the Task11 directory:

    `DIR SALARY.*` `ENTER`

Make a copy of the file called SALARY.JAN

    `COPY SALARY.FEB SALARY.JAN` `ENTER`
    `DIR SALARY.*` `ENTER`

Make another copy of the file called SALARY.MAR, but copy this one to the root directory:

    `COPY SALARY.FEB \ SALARY.MAR` `ENTER`
    `DIR \ SAL*.*` `ENTER`

Notice that you can copy within the same directory but to a destination file with a different name, or you can copy a file or files to a different directory retaining the original name as you did earlier in Task 7, or with a new name, as you have just done.

Activity 11.2   Copying more than one file and changing the names

Spreadsheets often make workfiles with an extension called .wks

You want to make duplicate files ending in .wk1 because you are going to work on a number of versions of the files:

1   `copy *.wks *.wk1` ENTER
       `dir *.wk?` ENTER
2 Make another set of the same files ending .wk2
3 Now **copy** all the .mem files so that the new files all have the ending .msg

---

Renaming files   If you want to change the name of the file without making a duplicate copy, you should rename it using the **ren** command.

Activity 11.3   Renaming a single file

There is a file called SALARY.90 and you want to call it SALARY.89

    `dir s*.90` ENTER
    `ren salary.90 salary.89` ENTER
    `dir salary.*` ENTER

Rename chq.wks to CHEQUE.WKS by typing:

    `ren chq.wks cheque.wks` ENTER
    `dir chq.wks` ENTER

DOS should return the error message 'File not found' because you are no longer creating duplicate files with different names.

Activity 11.4   Renaming groups of files

Rename all files ending .txt so that they end .asc

    `dir *.txt` ENTER
    `ren *.txt *.asc` ENTER
    `dir *.asc` ENTER

Rename all files beginning **cm** so they begin with **zz** and end with **.new**

    `dir cm*.*` ENTER
    `ren cm*.* zz*.new` ENTER
    `dir *.new` ENTER

You will probably get an error message if you successfully completed Activity 11.2.

Activity 11.5	Further practice
	1 Rename all the .dat files to .bak
	2 Copy SALARY.FEB to SALARY.MAY
	3 Rename SALARY.FEB SALARY.OCT.

Key words	**Copy**
	Rename

Task 12   Setting a path

Objective

To set up a path so that programs can be accessed outside the home directory.

Instructions

So far you have been using the internal DOS commands that are loaded into memory whenever the computer is booted up. This means that you may execute these commands from any subdirectory in your particular system and expect them to work.

So-called 'external' commands are supplied as programs on a floppy disk and can be copied onto the hard disk if the computer has one. You have to be logged into the drive and directory where an external command program is located to be able to run the program. External command programs can be additional DOS commands and utilities, applications software or programs you write yourself.

To illustrate this you will create a simple program called task.bat. Creating batch file programs is covered in more detail in Section E, but this example is very easy to set up.

Activity 12.1

Creating a simple **batch** program

A batch file is a list of commands that can be executed automatically by submitting a batch, or list of them, for processing.

First make a new subdirectory called TASK12, then move to it:

> md task12 `ENTER`
> cd task12 `ENTER`

Then make the program file using **copy con** as you did in Task 8:

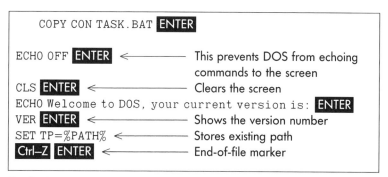

```
     COPY CON TASK.BAT  ENTER

ECHO OFF  ENTER   ←——————  This prevents DOS from echoing
                            commands to the screen
CLS  ENTER   ←——————  Clears the screen
ECHO Welcome to DOS, your current version is:  ENTER
VER  ENTER   ←——————  Shows the version number
SET TP=%PATH%   ←——————  Stores existing path
Ctrl–Z  ENTER   ←——————  End-of-file marker
```

Finally, to run your program, type:

> task `ENTER`

When the program is executed it will clear the screen, display the welcome line, tell you the version number and then store the current path in a memory workspace, or variable called **TP** (Temporary Path).

Activity 12.2   Investigating the current path

Move back to the root directory, and type the name of your program again:

```
cd \ ENTER
task ENTER
```

```
Bad command or filename
```

DOS cannot run your program because you are in the root directory and your program is in another directory. It is inconvenient to have to move to a directory where a program is located before you can run it. You can set up a path in the computer's memory that will be searched if the program cannot be found in the current directory.

To see if a path has already been set up, type:

```
path ENTER
```

If there is none, the message 'No path' will be returned, otherwise you will see something like this:

```
PATH C:\ ;C:\DOS;C:\UTILS;C:\WIN;
```

First DOS will search the root directory ———
Next the \DOS directory ———
Then the \UTILS directory ———
Finally the \WIN (windows) directory ———

Notice that each part of the path is separated from the next by a semicolon.

Activity 12.3   Setting a new path

First clear any currently set path by typing:

```
Set path= ENTER
```

Now if you type **path** on its own, the message 'No path' will be returned

Set the new path:

```
set path=B:\task12 ENTER
```

Now type the name of your program:

```
task ENTER
```

Activity 12.4   Restoring the original path

You stored the original path in a temporary workspace or variable called TP. To restore the path you will have to write another program which you can call SETPATH. Use **copy con** again:

```
copy con setpath.bat ENTER
```

```
SET PATH=%TP% ENTER
Ctrl–Z ENTER
```

Then run it by typing: `setpath` ENTER

Check that it has worked by typing: `path` ENTER

You will be learning some of the external DOS commands in Section C, so it will be important to know where they are located and also whether a path has been set to enable you to issue these commands from any other drive or directory.

Key words   **Set path**
                  Temporary path

Section C: External commands, new disks and security ▬▬▬▬▬

All the commands in this section are part of the set of **external commands** which will be supplied either on a systems disk located in drive A of a dual floppy system, or on the hard disk drive C. Users of networked machines should consult the network manager before proceeding with this section.

You will continue to use your practice disk in drive B, so a path will have to be set to whatever directory the DOS external commands are located in. Check this by typing PATH `ENTER` If the message 'no path' appears, try to set one up yourself. If the external commands are located in the directory C:\DOS then a suitable path would be C\;C:\DOS;

Task 13

Displaying the tree structure

Objectives

To use the **tree** command to show a directory structure.
To consolidate and practise the directory commands.

Instructions

In Section A, Task 5, you created a directory structure based on the filing system of an estate agent's office. You made directories with the command **md**, changed from one directory to another with **cd** and finally removed directories with **rd**, based on the structure shown in the diagram on p.12. When working on a computer, especially an unfamiliar one, you do not have such a mental picture to work from. You have to learn to visualise the directory tree structure by moving around it and using the **dir** command. This is like a worm's eye view of the system.

The **tree** command helps you to create more of a bird's eye view. We didn't use it before because it is an **external command**. You need to be able to work at the worm level in case utility programs such as **tree** are not available on the computer.

Activity 13.1

Preparing a new directory structure

Before you can try out the **tree** command you will have to re-create a new system of subdirectories. Make sure you are in the root directory of the practice disk in drive B, then type:

md user `ENTER`

md system `ENTER`

md data `ENTER`

This will make three new subdirectories at the level below the root directory.

Then change directory to USER by typing cd user `ENTER` and make two new user directories for JOE and SUE. When you've done that, change to the DATA directory and make three directories called MEMO, DOCS and ACCOUNTS.

(See Task 4 for detailed instructions if you have any difficulties.)

Activity 13.2   Using the **tree** command

Type `tree` **ENTER** and if you've created the directories correctly your list should look like the one below.

If you have a printer attached you can redirect the output of **tree** by adding the redirect sign '>' and the device name of the printer which is probably PRN, e.g.

    `tree >prn` **ENTER**

```
DIRECTORY PATH LISTING
Path: \ USER
Sub-directories:   JOE
                   SUE

Path: \ USER \ JOE
Sub-directories:   None

Path: \ USER \ SUE
Sub-directories:   None

Path: \ SYSTEM
Sub-directories:   None

Path: \ DATA
Sub-directories:   MEMO
                   DOCS
                   ACCS

Path: \ DATA \ MEMO
Sub-directories:   None

Path: \ DATA \ DOCS
Sub-directories:   None

Path: \ DATA \ ACCS
Sub-directories:   None
```

If you were looking at the listing on the screen, the first few lines probably scrolled off out of sight. You can use a DOS utility called **more** to display a screenful of data.

More prints `-------More-------` to remind you that there is more to come. Press any key to see the next screen, like dir/p.

    `TREE ¦ MORE` **ENTER**
                  the PIPE symbol ' ¦ 'connects the output of TREE to the input of MORE

The redirection symbol '>' and the pipe symbol ' ¦ ' are explained in Section E.

Displaying filenames within the tree structure

Change to the root directory and copy the following files to the subdirectories as instructed:

1 All files ending in .EXE and .COM to \SYSTEM
2 All the .DAT files to \DATA
3 All the .DOC and .TXT files to \DATA\DOCS
4 The ADMIN and ACCOUNT files to the ACCOUNTS subdirectory
5 Files ending .MEM to the MEMO subdirectory.

If you need help turn to Task 7.

Now use the **tree** command again, this time using the /f switch which displays a list of files inside directories.

TREE / F | MORE `ENTER` (or `tree/f>prn if you have a printer`)

Your listing should look similar to the section of the DIRECTORY PATH LISTING shown here:

```
Path: \USER\SUE
Sub-directories:  None

Files:            None


Path: \SYSTEM
Sub-directories:  None
Files             BTREE     .COM
                  BASIC     .COM
                  ADMIN     .COM
                  ACCOUNT   .EXE

Path: \DATA
Sub-directories:  MEMO
                  DOCS
                  ACCS

Files:            ACCOUNTS


Path: \DATA\MEMO
Sub-directories:  None

Files:            CMJOE     .MEM
                  CMSUE     .MEM
                  CMLIZ     .MEM
```

Troubleshooting

The most likely problem you may experience is that DOS cannot find the **tree** or **more** commands because a path to the DOS external commands has not been properly set up. Follow the instructions on p.42.

Activity 13.4   Further explorations

Try exploring the tree structures of other disks. The command is particularly useful in conjunction with a printer on computers with a hard disk. If you regularly use a hard disk machine you should print out the tree at the end of every week. This helps to locate files at a later date.

DOS 4 variations   The **tree** program has been greatly enhanced under Version 4 of DOS. This is output you get from the command:

```
Directory PATH listing
B:.
│   TEMP
│
├── USER
│   ├── JOE
│   └── SUE
├── SYSTEM
│       BTREE.COM
│       BASIC.COM
│       ADMIN.COM
│       NE.COM
│       TEMP
│
└── DATA
        ACCOUNTS.DAT
        SALES89.DAT

    ├── MEMO
    │       CMJOE.MEM
    │       CMSUE.MEM
    │       CMLIZ.MEM
    ├── DOCS
    │       HELP.DOC
    │
    └── ACCOUNTS
            ADMIN.EXE
            ADMIN.COM
```

This graphical tree structure really does provide a bird's eye view of the directory structure.

A number of utility packages such as **pc tools**, **dtree** and so on can be used to provide this type of display.

Do not try to copy **tree** from a computer which has DOS 4 installed on it. Unless you are able to install DOS 4 entirely, individual enhanced utilities such as **tree** will not run. All you will see is the error message:

```
Incorrect DOS version
```

Key words   Tree
Path
More

Task 14   **Background printing**

Objectives   To print text file(s) as a background process.
To learn more about the concept of 'multi-tasking'.

Instructions   More often than not you will create printed output from within a software package such as a wordprocessor. If you have a printer on-line to your computer, you will already have seen that it is possible to print the contents of a file by copying it to the print device, e.g. `copy readme.txt prn`
or by re-directing the output of a command as in the previous task, e.g. `tree >prn`

If you have a number of long files to print, it is often more efficient to use the **print** command, because you can continue to use the computer to do other things while it processes your print jobs automatically.

Activity 14.1   Creating a file to print

First make a text file by redirecting the output of the tree command into a file you can call TREE.LIS. Use TREE.LIS to experiment on.

`tree /F >TREE.LIS` ENTER
└───────────────────── Use the greater than sign '>'

Check that this has worked by typing:

`TYPE TREE.LIS` ENTER

The contents of the file should have been displayed; it will appear just as if you had typed **tree** in the first place!

Make sure that the printer is ready and copy the file to the printer, noting what happens. There will be a short time before the computer is ready for you to type another command. Enter the two commands below, one immediately after the other.

`copy TREE.LIS PRN` ENTER

`TREE.LIS` ENTER

This method of printing is called **foreground printing** because the computer regards the task of copying data between two devices as a primary or foreground task. It will not process the next command until printing is completed. The effect of this is likely to be somewhat diminished if your printer has 'buffer' memory. This enables the printer to store data to be printed so that it can pass control back to the computer while it prints data from the buffer at its own speed.

Activity 14.2   Printing the same file in the background

Note: **print** is another external command, so if you get the Bad command or filename error it is because the path is not set correctly. See note on p.3.

Step 1   Set up the printer by typing:

    `print` `ENTER`

The computer will respond:

```
Name of list device [PRN:] ENTER
Resident part of PRINT installed
PRINT queue is empty
```

Press enter to acknowledge the default setting

Step 2   Now type:

    `print TREE.LIS` `ENTER`

Then immediately type:

    `dir` `ENTER`

This time the prompt should come back to you quite quickly, and you will be able to process the command **dir** almost immediately.

Activity 14.3   Setting up a print queue

You can submit many files to the list device and the command **print** deals with them in the order in which they arrive. A program that manages a print queue in this way is called a **spooler**. This is an important feature of a multi-user operating system where one printer has to handle any number of simultaneous requests. You will find that experiments with printer queues tend to use up rather a lot of paper.

Try printing all the .mem files:

    `print *.mem` `ENTER`

You may find that a blank sheet appears between each file.

Activity 14.4   Adding more files to the print queue

So as not to waste too much paper, take the printer off-line or switch it off. If you do not have a printer you can still try this experiment:

    `print A*.*` **ENTER**

All files beginning with the letter A should now be in the print queue. Ignore any messages telling you that there is no list device present. Add some more files by typing:

    `print M*.*` **ENTER**

At some stage an error will appear saying 'Print queue is full'. You will notice that 10 files are in the queue when this happens. The switch /q sets the number of files that can be held in the queue. The minimum number is 4, the maximum is 32 and the default setting is 10.

    `print /q:24` **ENTER**
    `print c*.*` **ENTER**

Activity 14.5   Removing files from the queue

If you decide that you do not want to print a file that is already in the queue, you can remove it by typing:

    `print admin.bat /c` **ENTER**

Notice that the /c cancel switch goes after the filename. This is called a **trailing switch**.

Display the queue by typing `print` **ENTER** then pick a file and remove it by including the /c switch. You can remove a group of files by using the wild '*' characters, thus:

    `print c*.* /c` **ENTER** will remove all files beginning with C.

You can exterminate the whole queue in one move by using the /t (terminate) switch:

    `print /t` **ENTER**

Advanced activities

DOS is normally thought of as a single-user, single-tasking operating system. The print command with its spooling capability can give some useful insights into some key ideas to do with multi-tasking.

Since the **print** command is loaded into memory, and can run in the background while another program runs in the foreground, it should be possible to optimise the way the command handles the spool queue by controlling the CPU **and memory** resources it uses.

There are two groups of switches for use with the command **print**. The leading switches control the way the command is configured, while the trailing switches act on the files to be spooled.

The general syntax of the command is thus:

```
print      [/1:] [path and filename] [/2]
   ┌─┘      |    └──┘               |      |
command  space  leading        file(s)   trailing
                switch                    switch
```

The first set of switches specify the list device and CPU resources allocated to the command. Notice that there is a colon after the switch which separates it from the data associated with that switch. You can include more than one leading switch.

These are the leading switches:

Switch	Name	Example	Function (DOS 4)
/d:	device:	/d:lpt2	sends output to the second parallel port, LPT2. Default is PRN, serial ports addressed as COM1 to 4
/b:	buffer	/b:1024	sets the size of the internal memory buffer in the computer. Default 512, range 1 to 1634
/u:	value1	/u:255	sets the number of clock ticks while **print** waits for printer to be on-line. Default 1, range 1 to 255
/m:	value2	/m:1	Specifies the number of clock ticks print takes to print a character. Default 2, range 1 to 255
/s:	slice	/s:16	The interval of time used by the DOS scheduler for the print command. Default 8, range 1 to 255

The following two leading switches are used after the print command but without any filenames:

/q:	queue	/q:24	The number of files that can be held in the spool queue. Default 8, range 4 to 32
/t	terminate	/t	Removes all files from the queue

50

There are only two trailing switches:

Switch	Example	Function
/c	print cm.bat /c	removes a file from the spool queue
/p	print pg.doc /p	switches on print mode if not already on and prints any files specified in the command line

If you are printing in the background, foreground processing can be adversely affected, particularly if the foreground process makes great demands on the processor and memory.

The amount of resources 'grabbed' by the background process **print** can be controlled by the values assigned to the leading switches.

The print command can be speeded up by giving it a larger memory buffer, (/b:). This could be at the expense of memory required by a foreground process. The two switches /m: and /s: control the scheduling of the CPU to the process.

In order to see the effect of re-allocating resources to the **print** process, you should try tuning the spooler program by assigning values to the switches as follows:

Activity 14.6   Assigning switch values

First you could try to force the spooler as far into the background as possible. You should run another process as soon as possible after issuing the **print** command. If you are a computer studies student, it might be an idea to write a short program that sets the clock, executes a simple loop 1000 times and then reads the clock again. Then you can run your program on its own to see how long it takes, then try it again after changing the settings of the spooler command.

To force the spooler into the background you could try:

```
print /m:255/s:255/q:32 ENTER
```

then submit some files. For example make up a list like this:

```
tree >tree.lis ENTER
dir a*.* >a.lis ENTER
dir *.doc >docs.lis ENTER
```

Now put them into the spool queue:

```
print *.lis ENTER
```

then immediately run your program.

Finally try tweaking up the print command to see if this has the effect of slowing down execution of the foreground process. You will probably have realised that the settings are critical to the fine tuning of a network server that handles printer spooling for a number users on the network.

If you increase the efficiency of the spooler, other processes running on the server will be slowed down. If the spooler is pushed too far into the background, users will start to complain that it takes forever to get a listing. The manager's job is to strike a balance, taking into account the type of work that the system has to do.

Key words	**Print**
	Tree
	Spool

Task 15   **Formatting a new disk**

Objectives

To format a floppy disk.
To re-boot the computer.
To minimise the risks of destroying data.

Instructions

New floppy disks are usually supplied unformatted in boxes of ten. Before they can be used in the computer to store programs or data they have to be formatted. This process creates an invisible pattern of magnetic tracks on the disk, together with an empty directory and a table called the **file allocation table** which assigns disk space to each file as it is created, updated and finally, deleted.

DOS will not recognise a floppy disk which is either unformatted or has been formatted by another operating system. For instance, disks from Apple micro-computers, BBC micros and Ataris cannot be used in an IBM compatible computer.

You will not be able to use this command if you are working at a diskless workstation on a network.

You are likely to come across two disk formats called normal density and high density. This is the case no matter whether your machine uses 3½ inch or 5 inch disks.

Activity 15.1

Formatting a normal density disk (48 tpi)

Warning! The format command destroys any data which may already exist on a disk.

The worst mistake you can make is to format the hard disk by accident, or more likely, through sheer carelessness. If you are in any doubt about whether you have typed the command correctly, ask your tutor or manager before pressing `ENTER`.

If you follow the simple instructions below, you should have no trouble at all. There are separate instructions for use on computers with different drive configurations.

Computers with a hard disk

Log onto the hard disk by typing:

    `C:` `ENTER`

Insert the new unformatted disk into the floppy drive A and close the latch.

Type the command:

    `format a:/4` `ENTER`
        ↑
        └──────────── make sure you include the drive letter a:

Once the process begins the output you see on screen tells you what is happening.

The /4 switch tells the machine to format the disk to normal 40 track density. This is only necessary if you have a machine with a high capacity floppy disk drive.

Computers with no hard disk

Take the system disk containing the DOS utilities and check that the write protect label is correctly in place. Place the system disk in drive A and type:

```
A: ENTER
```

Now place the new unformatted disk in drive B and close the latch. Do not attempt to log onto drive B. To start formatting, type:

```
format b:/4 ENTER
```

If your machine has only one floppy drive you will be prompted to replace the source disk with the target disk. The source disk which must be write-protected is the one containing DOS system files; the target disk is the one you want to format.

The format command messages

Whichever machine you have, when formatting has completed, a message like this should appear:

```
362496 bytes total disk space
362496 bytes available on disk
```

This means that the disk has successfully been formatted to normal density enabling 360K bytes of storage.

Possible errors will result in the following messages being displayed onscreen.

```
Bad command or filename
```

See the note on p.3.

```
Format failure Disk fault error
```

The disk you are trying to format is not compatible, or has surface faults. Discard it.

When reformatting old disks it is wise to check them with DIR. If you get a read error it may be because the disk belongs to a different computer such as a BBC micro. Take care before formatting unknown disks in case they contain someone else's vital data.

Activity 15.2

High density format and volume labels

If your computer is an IBM compatible 'AT' type with an 80286 or an 80386 processor, the chances are it will have a high capacity floppy disk drive capable of formatting 96tpi disks to the 80 track high density standard. You can try the command in the form given below even if your machine can only accept disks formatted to 40 tracks. It will continue to format at normal density by default.

```
format a:/v:PRACTICE2 ENTER
```

The /v: switch followed by the volume label will write the label 'PRACTICE2' onto the disk to help you identify it at a later date.

After formatting the disk the standard report on the disk space available will look similar to this:

```
1213952 bytes total disk space
 307200 bytes in bad sectors
 906752 bytes available on disk
```

This is probably because you have used a 48tpi disk instead of a high density 96tpi disk. If fewer than 100 000 bytes are available you should reformat the disk using the /4 switch. You will find the disk behaves unreliably if it has too many bad sectors. An unwelcome sign is that formatting begins to slow down progressively after cylinder 50.

Activity 15.3   Creating a BOOT disk

By using the /s switch you can create a new disk which can be used to boot the computer from the A drive. This time you can use several switches together. For added reliability create a system disk using 360K format. You can include the volume label switch, but this time do not include it in the command line. You will be prompted for it when the format process is complete.

The exact screen display produced by DOS 3.3 is shown here:

format a:/4/s/v ENTER

```
Insert new diskette for drive A:
and strike ENTER when ready
ENTER
Head:           0      Cylinder:       39
System transferred

Volume label (11 characters, ENTER for none)? DOS3.3

Invalid characters in volume label
Volume label (11 characters, ENTER for none)? DOSv3

    362496 bytes total disk space
        78848 bytes used by system
        283648 bytes available on disk
```

Notice that the volume label cannot contain illegal filename characters (see p.ix).

| **Testing your boot disk: Re-booting the computer** | To test out your new boot disk you need to reset the computer. Read the following section before attempting the re-boot: |

There are two ways of resetting a computer.

1 Cold boot

Switch off the computer, pausing for a few moments until disk drive activity has ceased, then switch on again.

2 Warm boot

Press the reset button, if there is one, or hold down the `Ctrl` and `Alt` keys together and press the `Del` (delete) key.

Warning! PARK the drive heads

If your computer has a hard disk you should always run the head park program before shutting off the power. This removes the heads from the drive surface. Normally this is done only if the computer is to be moved. When the machine is powered up, whether it has been moved or not, electrical disturbances can progressively corrupt the disk and shorten its effective life.

The head park program does not have a standard name because it is not supplied as a standard MS-DOS command. Typical examples are PARK, DPARK, SHIPDISK.

Activity 15.4

Warm boot

You should always be able to force a warm boot by holding down `Ctrl` `Alt` and pressing `Delete` even if the computer has a reset button.

Place your newly created system disk in drive A:

```
A: ENTER
DIR ENTER
```

Dir should show you that the file command.com has been transferred to the disk. Now hold down the

`Ctrl` and `Alt` keys together and press `Del`

When the computer boots up you will be asked to set the date and time, see Activity 1.1 on p.2.

Activity 15.5   Restoring everything to normal

Remove your boot disk and replace it in its dust cover. If you are working on a floppy disk machine, you should replace the master system disk in drive A.

If the machine has a hard disk, there should not be a diskette in the floppy disk drive.

Press `Ctrl` `Alt` `Delete` again, and the computer will boot up in the normal way.

Key words   Format
`Ctrl` `Alt` `Delete`

Task 16

Copying an entire disk

Objective

To copy the contents of one floppy disk to another.

Instructions

The external command **diskcopy** copies the contents of the floppy disk in the source drive to a formatted or unformatted disk in the target drive. In the case of a single disk drive machine DOS will tell you which disk to put into the drive.

Warning! All data on the target disk will be lost, so you should afford this command the same degree of respect as you did the **format** command. **Diskcopy** works only with floppy disks; you cannot use it with a hard disk.

You will use your practice disk as the source disk. The disk you formatted in the previous task can be used as the target disk. Alternatively you can use a new unformatted disk.

Activity 16.1

Diskcopy on a computer with a hard disk and one floppy drive

Fix a write-protect tab on to the source disk before inserting it in the floppy drive, then type:

    A: `ENTER`

    diskcopy a: b: `ENTER`

This is how it should look on your screen:

a: \ >diskcopy a: b: `ENTER`

Insert SOURCE diskette in drive A:
Press any key when ready . . . `ENTER`

Copying 40 tracks
9 sectors/track, 2 Side(s)

Insert TARGET diskette in drive A:
Press any key when ready . . . `ENTER`

Copy another diskette (Y/N)?n `ENTER`

Activity 16.2 **Diskcopy** on a machine with two floppy disk drives

The two drives must match so you cannot attempt a diskcopy from a 5 in. drive to a 3½ in. drive. You can **diskcopy** from a normal capacity drive of the same size to a high capacity drive but not the other way round.

Place the system disk in drive A:

```
a: ENTER
diskcopy a:b:
```

Remove the system disk and return it to its cover then place the write-protected source disk in drive A and the target disk in drive B. Press any key to continue when instructed.

Activity 16.3 **Diskcopy** on machine with one floppy drive only

Place the system disk in the floppy drive and type:

```
diskcopy a:b: ENTER
```

Remove the system disk and return it to its cover then follow the instructions by placing the write-protected source disk in the drive and swapping it with the target disk when you are told to do so.

Diskcopy works out the number of tracks, sides and sectors it has to copy by reading data on the source disk. If your computer has less memory than the capacity of the disk, you will have to swap the two disks several times over.

As a general rule, you should find out whether the source disk was formatted to the normal or high density standard and then supply a suitable target disk. If you supply a normal density target disk and attempt to copy from a high density source disk you will lose data and your files will probably be corrupted.

Key words	Diskcopy

Task 17   Protecting files

Objectives

To protect files from accidental or deliberate erasure.
To set the archive flag.

Instructions

Each file can have two attributes associated with it:

1 The read-only attribute determines whether you may update or delete the file.

2 The archive flag determines whether the file is selected for backing up by the **Backup** and **xcopy** commands.

Activity 17.1

Setting a file to read only

Create a file on your practice disk called special.doc, check its default attributes, set it to read-only status and then try to update it, as follows:

b: `ENTER`

echo File to test the attrib command >special.doc `ENTER`

type special.doc `ENTER`

attrib special.doc `ENTER`

echo which can protect your files >>special.doc `ENTER`

type special.doc `ENTER`

attrib +r special.doc `ENTER`

echo try to add another line >>special.doc `ENTER`

Notice that you redirected the phrase following the command echo into the file special.doc by means of the redirect '>' symbol. You can append another line of text to the same file by using two greater than '>>' symbols.

The default settings are: read only OFF
archive ON

To set the read only attribute to ON use the +r switch. This should prevent you from echoing the additional line to the file. You should see the error message:

Access denied.

Activity 17.2   Using wild characters with **attrib**

Display the current attributes of all files by typing:

    `attrib *.*` **ENTER**

You can protect all files in a directory by typing:

    `attrib +r b:\ *.*` **ENTER** [normal rules about wild characters apply]

Now try deleting all the files:

    `del b:\ *.*` **ENTER**

    `Access denied`

Would you want to protect all files in a given directory? Think about this before turning to p.121.

Activity 17.3   Changing the archive flag

The **xcopy** and **backup** commands (see Tasks 18 and 19) inspect the archive flag to determine whether the file should be included in a general backup operation.

You will have already discovered that a newly created file has the archive flag set ON by default. However, the user can reset the flag to OFF if the file is not required to be backed up.

Look at the attributes of the file SPECIAL.DOC

    `attrib special.doc` **ENTER**

You should see that both archive and read only flags are ON

Remove them both by typing:

    `attrib -a-r special.doc` **ENTER**
    `attrib special.doc` **ENTER**

Now update the file by adding another line:

    `echo more stuff >>special.doc` **ENTER**
    `attrib special.doc` **ENTER**

The archive attribute has been automatically reset to ON by the action of updating the file. Consider the usefulness of this: by controlling the archive flag, only those files which have been updated need to be selected for backing up. These ideas will be explored further in Task 18.

Summary:
Command syntax

The general form of the command is:

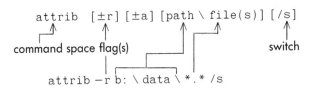

+r sets the read only attribute
−r removes the read only attribute
+a sets the archive attribute or flag
−a removes the archive flag

If no flags are specified in the command, **attrib** will merely display the attributes of the files in the specified or default path.

The /s switch processes all subdirectories below the specified path. You can test this by changing to the root directory of your practice disk and typing

```
attrib *.*/s
```

Key words	**Attrib**
	Backup
	Xcopy

Task 18　　Backing up subdirectories

Objectives　　To learn different ways of making secure back-ups of both files and directory structures. To be able to decide on the most appropriate method to use.

Instructions　　**Note: Xcopy** is available on DOS version 3.3 and later versions.

You have already learnt two commands that can be used to backup data; the internal command **copy** and the external command **diskcopy**.

Copy can be used satisfactorily to make backup copies of the files individually, or by using the wild characters if the files have a common pattern of characters in their names. If you need to copy a whole range of different filenames from various subdirectories whose only common property is, for instance, that they have all been created or updated since the same time yesterday, you will have to change directories, identify the right files and type in the **copy** command several times in each subdirectory to do it.

In DOS 3.3 and subsequent versions there is a more sophisticated **copy** command, called **xcopy** (i.e. eXternal copy command).

The additional features of **xcopy** enable you to copy:

- both files and whole directory structures
- files which have their archive flag set
- files created or modified on or after a specified date
- directory structures between disks of different formats (as opposed to **diskcopy**)

Activity 18.1　　Copying a directory structure

You will need your practice disk and the new disk you formatted in Task 15.

Hard disk users should insert the practice disk containing the directory structure you created in Task 13 to illustrate the **tree** command.

Copy the tree structure from the branch \ DATA downwards, including any files in the directory DATA itself and its 'child' subdirectories MEMO, DOCS and ACCOUNTS.

Log onto the practice disk as drive A by typing:

    `a:` ENTER

Change to the DATA directory by typing:

    `cd \ data` ENTER

Then type:

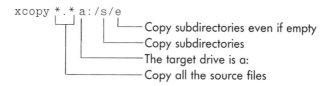

You may be prompted to change disks several times.

Command syntax	The general syntax of the command is:

xcopy [*source drive:files*] [*target drive: files*] [*switches*]

If you do not specify the target parameters **xcopy** will copy from the specified source to the drive you are currently logged onto, i.e. the default directory.

Activity 18.2	Copying files using the archive flag

There are two switches that involve the archive flag, see Task 17, p.61.

/a   **xcopy** copies only those files whose archive flag is set ON

/m   Same as the /a switch except that after copying the file(s) it resets the archive flag to OFF

With the practice disk in drive B, change to the \ SYSTEM subdirectory. The files you created in Activity 13.3 should still be there. Check their attributes by typing:

```
cd \system
attrib *.* ENTER
```

All the archive flags will set ON by default. Remove the archive flag from the files ending .com

```
attrib −a *.com ENTER
```

Copy the files to the DATA \ ACCOUNTS subdirectory:

```
xcopy *.* \data\accounts /a ENTER
```

Which files were copied?

Now reset the archive flag by typing:

```
attrib +a *.* ENTER
```

then copy the files using the /m switch:

```
xcopy *.* \data\accounts /m ENTER
attrib *.* ENTER
```

Notice that the **xcopy** operation has caused the archive flags to be switched OFF. They will be switched ON again only when files are updated, or the user intervenes. By using the /m switch and **xcopy** regularly, you can backup only those files which have changed since the last backup.

Activity 18.3　　　　Using **xcopy** and the date switch

Check the date, then create a new file which will be date stamped so that you can test the **xcopy** date switch.

date **ENTER**　Press **ENTER** if the date displayed is correct, or type in the correct date in the format shown

```
echo Activity 17.3 >example.tmp ENTER
dir *.tmp ENTER
xcopy *.* \data /d:date ENTER
```

You must type in the date in the correct format, here

This is another way in which the backup process could be controlled. New files or files which have been amended will have had their date stamp altered since the date of the last backup. Remember that the date switch causes **xcopy** to copy files on or after the specified date.

Other switches:　　/p　　prompts the user with '(Y/N)' to confirm whether the target file is to be created

　　　　　　　　　　/v　　verifies that the target file(s) are indeed identical to the source file(s)

　　　　　　　　　　/w　　waits before copying files. **Xcopy** displays the message:
　　　　　　　　　　　　　`press any key when ready to start copying files`

Key words	Xcopy
	Copy

Task 19   **Making a backup disk**

Objective

To back up one or more files from one disk to another.

Instructions

Although there are certain similarities between **backup** and **xcopy**, there are nevertheless reasons why you would use **backup** as opposed to **xcopy**. For instance:

- The machine may not have DOS 3.3 or a later version installed in which case **xcopy** will not be available.
- The space on the target disk may be too small for the number of files on the source disk.

In most circumstances, users will require the hard disk or parts of it to be backed up to floppy disk(s). When the target floppy diskette is full, **backup** will prompt you to load another diskette, then another and so on, until all the files on the source drive have been copied.

The companion program is called **restore** which reads the header track on the first backup disk of a session and will prompt you to load the remaining diskettes in the correct sequence. You should label and number each backup disk in that sequence so as to restore the files properly at a later date.

Activity 19.1   Making a backup disk

Unless you are working on a machine with a hard disk there is no advantage in using this command as opposed to one of the other commands described above.

Warnings!
- The target disk should be a new disk, as **backup** will erase any existing files in the root directory. A warning message telling you that this is about to happen will be displayed.
- You cannot use an old version of DOS to restore files backed up with the DOS 4 backup command.
- If the source disk to be backed up is a 5 in. floppy diskette, always affix a write protect tab or in the case of a 3½ in. disk set the plastic switch to the read only position.
- If you are working on a diskless network station, consult the network manager before attempting to use this command.

Command syntax and switches

The general syntax is:

> **backup** [*source*] [*target*] [/*switches*]

Both source and target can consist of any combination of drive letter, path and filename(s) or wild characters:

`a:`	All files in the root directory of a:
`a:\user\*.dat`	Only the .dat files in subdirectory \user on the a: drive

---

The **backup** command switches will be familiar from those you have already come across, particularly with **xcopy**.

Switch	Function
/a	Adds files to be backed up to those already on the backup disk. Old backup files will not be erased.
/d:date	Backs up files updated or created on or after that date.
/t:time	Backs up files updated on or after the specified time.
/f	Formats an unformatted target disk.
/f:size	Formats the target disk to the specified size, e.g. s:360, s:1.2 (DOS v4 only)
/L:file	Logs a backup entry in the specified file. By default, i.e. if you don't specify a filename the /L switch will place a file called backup.log in the root directory of the sourcefile disk.
/m	Backs up only those files changed since the last backup. See the notes on **attrib** and **xcopy**, pp.61 and 62.
/s	Backs up subdirectories below the specified or default path.

Example 1

```
backup c:\user\sue a:
```

Backs up all files in the \user\sue subdirectory on drive C to a blank, formatted disk in drive A.

Example 2

```
backup c:\user a:/s/m
```

Backs up files that have changed since the last backup in directory c:\user and subdirectories below.

**Example 3
(DOS v4)**

```
backup c:\user b:/f:360
```

Backs up the C drive directory to an unformatted 360Kbyte floppy in drive B.

Example 1

```
c: \ >backup c:\user\ sue a:

Insert backup diskette 01 in drive A:

Warning! Files in the target drive
A: \ root directory will be erased
Strike any key when ready

*** Backing up files to drive A: ***
Diskette Number: 01

\ USER \ SUE \ AUTOEXEC.BAT
\ USER \ SUE \ WP.BAT
\ USER \ SUE \ WORD.BAT
\ USER \ SUE \ NEW-VARS.BAT
\ USER \ SUE \ W.BAT
\ USER \ SUE \ TASK.BAT
\ USER \ SUE \ PA.BAT


C: \ > dir a:

Volume in drive A is BACKUP 001
Directory of A: \

BACKUP     001          374        2-05-90   3:18p
CONTROL    001          447        2-05-90   3:18p
C               <DIR>              2-01-90   1:49p
     3 File(s)      354304 bytes free


C: \ >
```

Example 2

```
C: \ USER>
C: \ USER>dir

Volume in drive C is DISK1_VOL1
Directory of C: \ USER

    .                <DIR>              2-06-90   4:33p
    . .              <DIR>              2-06-90   4:33p
SUPPLIER   DBF          1146       10-13-89  11:36a
ITEMS      DBF          1434        2-06-90   4:35p
ORDERS     DBF          1066       10-13-89   3:55p
SUPPLIER   FMT           744       10-11-89  11:17a
ORDER      FRM          1997        2-06-90   4:34p
ORDERS1    FMT           298       10-11-89   1:42p
ORDTOP     FRM          1990       10-13-89   3:49p
     9 File(s)    22126592 bytes free
```

```
C: \ USER>backup a: c:/s/m

Insert backup source diskette in drive A:
Strike any key when ready

Warning! Files in the target drive
C: \ BACKUP directory will be erased
Strike any key when ready

*** Backing up files to drive C: ***
\ BACKUP.001
\ CONTROL.001

C: \ USER>dir

Volume in drive C is DISK1_VOL1
Directory of C: \ USER

    .                <DIR>              2-06-90   4:33p
    . .              <DIR>              2-06-90   4:33p
    SUPPLIER  DBF         1146     10-13-89  11:36a
    ITEMS     DBF         1434      2-06-90   4:35p
    ORDERS    DBF         1066     10-13-89   3:55p
    SUPPLIER  FMT          744     10-11-89  11:17a
    ORDER     FRM         1997      2-06-90   4:34p
    ORDERS1   FMT          298     10-11-89   1:42p
    ORDTOP    FRM         1990     10-13-89   3:49p
        9 File(s)    22114304 bytes free

C: \ USER>
```

Example 3

```
C: \ >
C: \ >backup c: \ qc2 \ v*.* a:/L

Logging to file C: \ BACKUP.LOG

Insert backup diskette 01 in drive A:

Warning! Files in the target drive
A: \ root directory will be erased
Strike any key when ready

*** Backing up files to drive A: ***
Diskette Number: 01

\ QC2 \ VARSIZE.C
\ QC2 \ VARSIZE.OBJ
\ QC2 \ VARSIZE.MDT
\ QC2 \ VARSIZE.ILK
\ QC2 \ VARSIZE.SYM
\ QC2 \ VARSIZE.EXE
```

```
C:\>
C:\>type \backup.log

2-5-1990  15:24:18  ←──────── First backup logged
001\USER\SUPPLIER.DBF
001\USER\ITEMS.DBF
001\USER\ORDERS.DBF
001\USER\SUPPLIER.FMT
001\USER\ORDER.FRM
001\USER\ORDERS1.FMT
001\USER\ORDTOP.FRM
2-5-1990  15:34:3  ←──────── Second backup added to the log
001\QC2\VARSIZE.C
001\QC2\VARSIZE.OBJ
001\QC2\VARSIZE.MDT
001\QC2\VARSIZE.ILK
001\QC2\VARSIZE.SYM
001\QC2\VARSIZE.EXE
```

Key words	Backup
	Restore

Task 20   **Restoring files from backup**

Objective

To **restore** files that have been backed up using the **backup** program.

Instructions

The commands **backup** and **restore** are complementary. Having made a backup you should store the disk safely away from the computer so that, in case of serious damage, both the computer and the backup disks are not lost.

    If a disk drive crashes or some other mishap occurs that causes loss or corruption of files, you can repair the damage by using **restore**. Remember that **restore** works only with a disk that has data written to it by the **backup** command. Backups which have been made using **copy**, **diskcopy** and **xcopy** will have to be restored using **copy** or **xcopy**.

    Normally you would use **restore** to copy files from a backup floppy diskette to the hard disk.

    The general syntax of the command is similar to **backup**:

restore [backup drive letter:] [target drive:\ path] [/switch(es)]

```
restore a: c: /s
```

Activity 20.1

Restoring files from backup

In the example above, all files and subdirectories on the backup disk in drive A would be copied to drive C, starting from the root directory as no path has been given.

Command switches

At first sight the switches look almost identical to those associated with the **backup** command. Be careful as they produce very different results.

Switch	Restores...
/a:date	only files modified on or after the specified date
/b:date	only files modified on or before the specified date
/e:time	only files modified at or before the specified time
/L:time	only files modified at or later than the specified time
/m	only files modified or created since the last backup
/n	only those files that no longer exist on the target disk
/n	only those files that no longer exist on the target disk
/p	prompts user for permission to restore files that are read only or have changed since last backup
/s	subdirectories as well as files

More hints

You are advised to check that files have been properly restored by using **dir**. If the file is readable (i.e. not a .com, .exe .ovl or .sys file) check it with **type**.

Restore cannot restore hidden system files. If they have been erased from a disk they can be replaced by using the **sys** command.

It is best to use matching versions of **restore** and **backup**; i.e. if you backed up files under DOS 4, you cannot restore under DOS 3.1. On the other hand it is possible to restore files under, say, DOS 4 that were backed up under earlier DOS versions.

Examples and print-outs
Example 1

```
C:\>
C:\>dir user

Volume in drive C is DISK1_VOL1
Directory of C: \

File not found        ←——————— No \ user directory

C: \ >restore a: c:/s

Insert backup diskette 01 in drive A:
Strike any key when ready

*** Files were backed up 02-06-1990 ***

*** Restoring files from drive A: ***
Diskette: 01
\ USER \ SUPPLIER.DBF
\ USER \ ITEMS.DBF
\ USER \ ORDERS.DBF
\ USER \ SUPPLIER.FMT
\ USER \ ORDER.FRM
\ USER \ ORDERS1.FMT
\ USER \ ORDTOP.FRM


C:\>dir user

Volume in drive C is DISK1_VOL1
Directory of C: \ USER        ←——————— (Directory has been created by restore)
```

.		\<DIR>		2-06-90	4:33p
. .		\<DIR>		2-06-90	4:33p
SUPPLIER	DBF		1146	10-13-89	11:36a
ITEMS	DBF		1427	10-13-89	3:55p
ORDERS	DBF		1066	10-13-89	3:55p
SUPPLIER	FMT		744	10-11-89	11:17a
ORDER	FRM		1990	10-13-89	3:35p
ORDERS1	FMT		298	10-11-89	1:42p
ORDTOP	FRM		1990	10-13-89	3:49p

```
    9 File(s)    22126592 bytes free

C:\>
```

Example 2

```
C:>copy *.com \user\sue
COMMAND.COM
DPARK.COM
SETUP.COM
DTEDIT.COM                          Directory changed since the last backup as some
DTREE.COM                           files have been copied into \user\sue
    5 File(s) copied
C:\>backup c:\user\sue /s/m

Insert backup diskette 01 in drive A:

Warning! Files in the target drive
A:\ root directory will be erased
Strike any key when ready

*** Backing up files to drive A: ***
Diskette Number: 01

\USER\SUE\COMMAND.COM
\USER\SUE\DPARK.COM
\USER\SUE\SETUP.COM
\USER\SUE\DTEDIT.COM
\USER\SUE\DTREE.COM

C:\>dir\sue\
C:\>dir\user\sue

Volume in drive C is DISK1_VOL1
Directory of C:\USER\SUE
```

.		\<DIR>	2-05-90	2:52p	
. .		\<DIR>	2-05-90	2:52p	
AUTOEXEC	BAT	134	12-17-89	12:36p	
WP	BAT	34	11-28-89	11:29a	Backed up
WORD	BAT	33	12-21-89	5:33p	in Example 1
NEW-VARS	BAT	99	12-13-89	4:23p	
W	BAT	28	1-03-90	6:09a	
TASK	BAT	28	1-12-90	11:07a	
PA	BAT	18	1-12-90	11:47a	
COMMAND	COM	25307	3-17-87	12:00p	
DPARK	COM	463	8-14-87	11:53p	
SETUP	COM	19808	1-05-87	4:24p	Backed up
DTEDIT	COM	29863	8-23-88	6:59p	in Example 2
DTREE	COM	25201	8-23-88	6:59p	

```
    14 File(s)    22018048 bytes free
```

Key words	Restore
	Backup
	Sys

Task 21   **Checking a disk**

Objectives
To scan a disk and check it for errors; to recover lost data; to optimise disk performance.

Instructions
This very useful external command will display a status report on a given disk of any type, as well as error messages relating to possible corrupted files. If the /f switch is used, **chkdsk** will attempt to salvage files.

Activity 21.1

Checking out your practice diskette

Place the diskette in the drive in the usual way and type:

    chkdsk b: `ENTER`

If the disk is in good order, you should expect to see a status display looking something like this:

    Volume PRACTICE_DISK created Sep 10, 1990 4:10p

        362496 bytes total disk space
             0 bytes in 1 hidden files
          3072 bytes in 3 directories
        175104 bytes in 9 user files
        184320 bytes available on disk

        655360 bytes total memory
        595456 bytes free

If the disk is a 'boot' disk containing the system files which are so called 'hidden' files you would have seen the line: 53248 bytes in 2 hidden files.

Command syntax

    chkdsk [drive:] [path/file(s)] [/switches]
                          |_____|
                                  └──── optional ────┘

If you type a filename after the drive letter, **chkdsk** displays a status report for the file(s) as well as for the disk. You will use this later on to determine the efficiency of the disk.

The **/f** option fixes errors caused by files that have lost their end of file markers or that have bad entries in the **F**ile **A**llocation **T**able (FAT).

The **/v** option displays the name of each file on the disk.

Activity 21.2   Checking the hard disk

To report on the status of the hard disk, type

    `c:` `ENTER`

    `chkdsk c:` `ENTER`

There is a strong probability that there will be some bad sectors on the hard disk.
You will see this displayed in a line like this:

    `6144 bytes in bad sectors`

chkdsk cannot fix this as it only works on files that have become corrupted. You
will learn how to recover bad sectors later on. The most common cause of such
problems occurs when a file is left open because the computer is switched off while
the file is being processed.

Error messages   When a file is left open there is a possibility of the end of file marker being lost and
then the entry in the file allocation table (FAT) becomes invalid. If you have a disk
which contains a bad file allocation table with files in 'limbo', **chkdsk** will produce
output looking like this:

```
C:\ >chkdsk a:
Volume PRACTICE_DISK created Sep 21, 1990 2:21p

Errors found, F paramenter not specified
Corrections will not be written to disk.

64 lost clusters found in 1 chains.
Convert lost chains to files (Y/N)?N   ◄──── The answer no has
                                              been given
65536 bytes disk space
    would be freed
```

This problem was caused by opening a file in the wordprocessor and switching off
the computer while the wordprocessor was running. This is not a practice to be
recommended if the file is one you value!

If you run **chkdsk** on the same disk but using the /f switch this is what happens:

```
C: \ >chkdsk a:/f
Volume PRACTICE_DISK created Sep 21, 1990 2:21p

64 lost clusters found in 1 chains.
Convert lost chains to files (Y/N)?Y
```

```
   362496 bytes total disk space
   0 bytes in 1 hidden files
   3072 bytes in 3 directories
   109568 bytes in 8 user files
   65536 bytes in 1 recovered files      ←—— fixed!
   184320 bytes available on disk
   655360 bytes total memory
   595456 bytes free
```

If you typed N for no to the question 'Convert lost chains to files', **chkdsk** would free the lost blocks so that they could be reassigned to the FAT table, then the 'limbo' files would be lost for ever.

Warning: when files are recovered by **chkdsk** they do not reappear with their original names. Recovered files are given names of the type FILExxxx.CHK where xxxx is a number in the range 0000 to 9999, e.g. FILE0001.CHK

It is up to the user to determine what the file is and then rename it to its original name. Use the **type** command to see if the file consists wholly of ASCII characters. If the display causes wild things to happen to the screen, discard the file because a recovered program file is not to be trusted.

Trouble-shooting

Other **chkdsk** error messages you may come across include:

Cannot chdir to root – most probably a fatal error and the disk is unusable.

Cannot chkdsk a network drive – you can normally **chkdsk** the hard disk of a server in stand-alone mode only.

Disk error reading or writing FAT – the File Allocation Table is bad. Copy files to another disk for safety then use **chdsk** with the **/f** switch.

Invalid cluster, file truncated – this is a fatal error caused by an invalid pointer to the disk address where the data is supposed to be located. The **/f** switch will truncate the file to zero length which means that the name only will remain.

Probable non DOS disk, continue (Y/N) – type **N**

Processing cannot continue – not enough memory, probably because you have installed memory resident programs such as the wasteful WINDOWS.

Unrecoverable error in directory
Convert directory to file (Y/N)? if you answer **Yes**, **chkdsk** will try to convert the bad directory to a file. If you answer **No** you may not be able to read/write to that directory.

Activity 21.3   Recovering bad sectors

If **chkdsk** shows that there are bad sectors on a disk you can attempt to recover any lost data with the command **recover**.

The syntax is simple: recover [drive:] [path] filename

e.g.   recover a:

or   recover c:\ wp\ report.chm

DOS will attempt to read the files sector by sector noting the bad ones and not re-writing data to them.
If you have already noticed a diskette with bad sectors, you could try recovering files.
This is what you might see:

    C:\ FILES>recover a:

    Press any key to begin recovery of the file(s) on drive A:

    18 file(s) recovered

    C\ FILES>dir/w

    FILE0001.REC   FILE0002.REC   FILE0003.REC
    FILE0004.REC   FILE0005.REC   FILE0006.REC (etc)

Warning: like **chkdsk**, **recover** resurrects bad files into temporary filenames called FILExxxx.REC, e.g. FILE005.REC. Unless you have a very clear idea of what the original names of the lost files were, do not attempt to use recover on a whole disk in one operation. You will be faced with trying to rename a whole bunch of FILExxxx.REC files and you will not know where to start!

Optimising disk performance

You may have noticed that a heavily used disk drive gets slower as time goes on and as more files and data are stored on it. When there is plenty of space on the disk a file can be written onto a series of **contiguous**, or neighbouring, blocks. The next file will be written to the following block, and so on.

What happens if you now want to add more data to the first file? It may, by now, have a new file next door to it which will block its potential growth.

The file allocation table sorts this out by finding the next available free space and putting the rest of the file there. As old files are deleted this frees space, but the 'holes' that this creates may not be large enough for newer files if they are large ones. They will be distributed all over the disk in what are called non-contiguous blocks.

As soon as this starts to happen we say that the disk has become **fragmented**.

Activity 21.4   Checking for files with non-contiguous blocks

If you run **chkdsk** with the optional filename argument, a list of any files that spread across two or more non-contiguous blocks will be displayed. If you try this on your practice disk by typing the command:

```
chkdsk a:\*.*  ENTER   – you will probably get the message:

All specified files are contiguous
```

This is because the files are relatively small, and there has been no need for a file to invade non-contiguous blocks. On the hard disk, if you have one, things are probably very different. Try looking for a subdirectory where there is a heavy traffic in creating, updating and deleting files.

If you run dBASE III, there will probably be a directory called \ db3, or dbase3. This is what would happen if you tried to run **chkdsk** on a dBASE directory:

```
chkdsk c:\db3\*.dbf ENTER

C:\DB3\CUSTOMER.DBF
    Contains 2 non-contiguous blocks

C:\DB3\STOCK.DBF
    Contains 8 non-contiguous blocks

C:\DB3\ORDERS.DBF
    Contains 4 non-contiguous blocks
```

You will see that the disk is suffering from the dreaded **disk fragmentation**! Performance will slow down because the disk drive heads will have to move all over the surface to recover a file from its fragmented blocks.

Activity 21.5   Reorganising the filestore

There are various ways of reorganising the disk so that files can be reallocated to contiguous blocks. The simplest way to achieve this is by taking the following steps:

1 Backup the contents of the badly fragmented directory to floppy diskettes, using **xcopy** or **backup**.
2 Create a new directory which will be on another part of the hard disk. If there is not enough room you will need to perform step **3**.
3 Delete all the files in the original directory.
4 Restore the files to the new directory.
5 Test the new directory using **chkdsk**.

The task is made simpler and also more effective by using one of the DOS utilities programs which are generally available.

It is worth using **chkdsk** on a regular monthly basis, especially where there is heavy traffic. It is amazing that network managers usually fail to do this, and yet this is really one of their most important tasks, as users are nearly always complaining about the poor performance of the network. This is invariably due to fragmentation of the shared hard disk.

Key words	**Chkdsk**
	File Allocation Table (FAT)
	Recover
	Fragmentation

Section D: Setting up a system ▬▬▬▬▬▬

In this section you will look critically at the current system then explore some of the ways in which a system can be configured.

Task 22   Looking at the existing system

Objectives

To revise some of the commands covered earlier.
To explore the current settings.

Activity 22.1

Producing a report on the system

To produce a report on the system, check the following, producing a disk file called STATUS.RPT which can be printed out as a report:

1 The current version of DOS
2 The default date and time
3 Display the contents of the CONFIG.SYS file
4 Display the contents of the AUTOEXEC.BAT file
5 Display the current environment settings
6 Display the status of the hard disk and the number of bytes of RAM memory available
7 Display the directory structure and comment on the contents and organisation of the structure
8 Copy the completed file STATUS.RPT to the printer.

To see how the system has been set up you will need to refer to the various outputs from the commands: **ver date time set chkdsk type** and **tree**

There are various ways of doing this: you could use the `Print Screen` key to dump the contents of a VDU screen to the printer, or type `Ctrl–P` and echo all characters to the printer, but the favoured method is to redirect the output from the commands to the status.rpt file.

Try this for yourself before comparing your results with the suggestions and comments that follow.

Activity 22.2   Creating a status report on your system

The output from the following commands (with the possible exception of **time** and **date** can be redirected to a file called STATUS.RPT which could be tidied up using a wordprocessor or text editor. Do each command first without the redirection sign so that you can see the output, then press F3 and add the redirection (i.e. >>status.rpt), e.g.

```
c: ENTER   (Assuming you have a hard disk)
cd \ ENTER
```

```
echo STATUS REPORT ON OPUS PC V >status.rpt ENTER   substitute the name
                                                    or make of your
                                                    computer
```

This opens the file and writes a heading line.

```
ver ENTER
ver>>status.rpt ENTER
```

This will add the output of the command **ver** to the report. If the Version is 3.1 or earlier you should be considering upgrading to 3.3 or 4.

```
date ENTER
time ENTER
```

If the time and date are wrong, ask yourself, why? If there is a battery operated clock, maybe the battery needs replacing or you should run the SETUP program to reset the clock permanently. If the date and time are correct, redirect their output to the report file.

```
echo    *********CONFIG.SYS***********>>status.rpt ENTER
type    config.sys ENTER
type    config.sys>>status.rpt ENTER
```

This assumes config.sys is in the root directory; it might be an idea to use **dir** to ascertain this first!

```
echo *******CURRENT ENVIRONMENT SETTINGS******>>status.rpt
ENTER
set ENTER
set >>status.rpt
```

```
echo ********AUTOEXEC.BAT*********>>status.rpt ENTER
type autoexec.bat ENTER
type autoexec.bat>>status.rpt ENTER
```

```
echo ******HARD DISK and MEMORY STATUS*******>>STATUS.RPT ENTER
chkdsk c:\ *.* ENTER
chkdsk c:\ *.* >>status.rpt ENTER
```

```
echo ********DIRECTORY STRUCTURE********>>STATUS.RPT ENTER

dir \ *.* ENTER
dir \ *.*>>status.rpt ENTER
```

If the root directory scrolls off the screen, there are too many files in it! They should be reallocated to suitable subdirectories, or archived and deleted.

```
tree c: ENTER
tree c: >>status.rpt ENTER
```

The file STATUS.RPT can now be tidied up using a word processor or you can print it out as it stands. If you find that the file does not contain the output from all the commands it may be because you did not use the **append** '>>' symbol. If you miss out one of the two chevrons, the file will be initialised and previous output will be lost.

| Key words | Ver |
| | Status report |

Task 23   Virtual drives

Objectives

To substitute a drive letter for a path.
To assign a different letter to a drive.

The term **virtual** is often used in computing to mean a device that is not real. A virtual disk has no physical existence, but the operating system can be configured to regard blocks of RAM memory as if it were a disk (see Task 24). Other tricks involve **substituting** non-existent drive letters for a subdirectory or path, or **assigning** a different drive letter to an actual drive.

Instructions

When you created the directory structure for the estate agent's office you probably found that the very long pathnames were rather clumsy to manipulate. Unless you are using a network, it is possible to **substitute** a non-existent drive letter for one of these long pathnames.

Activity 23.1   Substituting a letter for a subdirectory

Step 1   Set up a new subdirectory on your practice disk:
Log onto the practice disk as drive B:

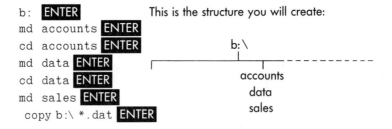

```
b:  ENTER          This is the structure you will create:
md  accounts ENTER
cd  accounts ENTER                      b:\
md  data ENTER
cd  data ENTER                  accounts
md  sales ENTER                 data
 copy b:\ *.dat ENTER           sales
```

You should now have a directory which will be used to store sales account data. The path is \ accounts\ data\ sales

Instead of having to refer to it by this long path, you could substitute a drive letter for it.

Step 2   Substitute the letter D for the path \accounts\ data\ sales

```
subst d: a:\accounts\ data\ sales
```

If the command worked, and this will depend on how your computer is configured, you can get into this directory simply by typing the virtual drive letter d:

```
d: ENTER
dir ENTER
Volume in drive D is
Directory of D:\

ACCOUNTS DAT    2443 31-12-89 7.17p
```

Problems when using subst

1 Choice of a suitable drive letter

You have to use a non-existent drive letter: you cannot substitute a letter which already relates to an actual drive on the system, or a letter that has already been used by **subst**.

If your machine already had a drive D in existence the **subst** command would fail. Supposing, for example, you tried substituting the letter S for Sales: it seems a logical choice and the letter is unlikely to conflict with an actual drive. Unfortunately the default setting accomodates drive letters in the range A–E only. You can alter this by including the statement

```
lastdrive=z
```

in the config.sys file. This is covered in Task 25.

2 Certain commands will not work on substituted drives. These include: **backup, restore, format, label, chkdsk, recover**

Try using **label** on your virtual drive. You may think it has worked, but later you will find that the *actual* disk containing the substituted path has been labelled!

Activity 23.2

Resetting the substituted drive

You can use the command on its own to report the presence of any virtual drives on the system.

subst **ENTER**

to remove a virtual drive, you end the command with the /d switch, e.g.

subst d: /d **ENTER**

Useful applications

Suppose you are developing a number of different applications using dBASE III. You can keep all the dBASE system files in a subdirectory called \db3. Branching down from that you may have applications for personnel management, order processing and a catalogue system.

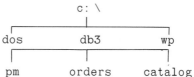

You could use the command **subst d: c:\db3\pm** before loading dBASE, then the dBASE command **SET DEFAULT TO D** will refer all disk operations to the virtual drive D, which is actually c:\db3\pm

Activity 23.3   Assigning a different letter to a drive

Before hard disks became commonplace applications software is often referred to the floppy drives A and B only. If you subsequently copied the software to a hard disk called C, the software would not run because it was trying to find its files on the floppy drives.

To run an application program that asks you to place the program disk in drive A and the data disk in drive B type the command:

```
assign a=c  b=c
```

Typing the command **assign** `ENTER` on its own resets the drives to their original letters.

You cannot use the following commands on drives that have had other letters assigned to them:

```
backup, restore, label, join, subst, print
```

General syntax of the commands   The **subst** command:

```
subst [drive 1:] [drive 2:] \ path
```

where `drive 1` is the **virtual** drive letter you want to substitute, and `drive 2` is the **actual** drive and pathname.

```
subst [drive:]/d
```

deletes the virtual drive that you specify in the argument.

The **assign** command:

```
assign [x] = [y]
```

where `[x]` is the name the application uses to address the drive
        `[y]` is the **actual** drive you want to address

A number of assignments can be made in one statement, as in the example:
```
assign a=c b=c
```

Key words   Subst
                 Assign

Task 24

Setting the environment

Objectives

To display the current environment; to set new environment variables; to configure the environment space;

Instructions

DOS reserves a part of memory for use as a reference area where information is stored about the way the computer has been set up. This area is called the **environment**.

You have already seen how the current settings can be displayed by using the command **set** on its own. Try it again:

set `ENTER`

A typical display might look like this:

```
comspec=c:\command.com
prompt $p$g
path=c:\;c:\dos;c:\utils
user=sue
home=c:\usr\sue
```

You have already come across the **prompt** and **path** commands. **Comspec** specifies the whereabouts of the **command processor** program, here located in the root directory of the C drive. Two other variables you are unlikely to see on your system are **user** and **home**. These may be defined by typing:

user=sue `ENTER`
home=c:\usr\sue `ENTER`

The system now knows that **sue** is the current user and that her home directory is **c:\ usr\ sue**. You will see the usefulness of this if you attempt the batch file programming exercise in Task 30.

Activity 24.1

Setting environment variables

Set up the variable **USER** with your name:

set user=[*name*] `ENTER`   substituting your own name or initials for [*name*]

To see if this has worked type: set `ENTER`

In the previous task you set up a directory called \accounts\data\sales. If this path is not already on your practice disk, turn back to Task 23 and create it now. Then type:

set home=b:\accounts\data\sales `ENTER`
set `ENTER`

The variable **home** can be used in batch files to perform various tasks such as writing data files to your home directory. Often these variables are set by the autoexec.bat program when the computer is first switched on.

The environment space

If you try to write too many variables into the environment you may get the error message:

```
Out of environment space
```

This can be adjusted by adding a line to the CONFIG.SYS file. Setting up the CONFIG.SYS file will be covered in Task 25.

Activity 24.2

Cancelling environment variables

To remove a variable from the environment, set it equal to the return key, i.e. nothing:

set `ENTER`
set user= `ENTER`
set `ENTER`

The general syntax of the **set** command is very simple:

```
set [variable]=[string]
```

where **variable** is the name you call the variable and **string** is the string of characters you assign to the variable. Used without any argument, **set** displays the current settings.

Key words   **Environment**
Set
Variable
String

Task 25

Configuring the system

Objective

To configure an IBM compatible computer to suit the user's requirements.

Instructions

In theory every user likes to have his or her computer set up in a way which reflects a personal working style, or optimised to suit their particular programs. In practice most users put up with configurations inherited from previous users, dealers or suppliers if the computer is new.

There are two types of configuration: **hardware** configuration and **software** configuration. The hardware configuration refers to the amount of memory (e.g. 640K), the processor (80286, 80386), what disk drives there are, their capacities and so on. The software configuration has to reflect this, but there are other features which need to be set up no matter what the hardware is.

You have already looked at some of the settings of your computer in Task 22. You will have found out which version of DOS is installed, whether the date and time are both accurately and permanently set, whether the file store has been sensibly structured into a coherent subdirectory system, whether the root directory contains the minimum number of system files or is overflowing with user files that should probably be somewhere else!

Most of these aspects of a system can be controlled by the use of commands you have already met. Does the keyboard behave the way you would expect it to? Do you get a pound sign when you press **SHIFT-3**, or do you get the 'hash' # sign? Are the " and @ keys reversed? Is the date shown in European or American format? These features are controlled by the autoexec.bat program together with the config.sys file.

When the computer boots up it reads statements in the config.sys file which tell it about system configuration, then the autoexec.bat file is executed which sets up further adjustments.

The config.sys file and what it affects

The config.sys file consists of a list of statements which enable various settings. A typical example of a config.sys might look like this:

```
BUFFERS=24
FILES=20
DEVICE=ANSI.SYS
SHELL=C:\COMMAND.COM /P /E:256
LASTDRIVE=Z
COUNTRY=44
```

The config.sys statements in more detail

BUFFERS=x e.g. BUFFERS=24

This statement tells DOS how much memory to reserve for **disk buffers** which are used to store data on its way to and from disk drives. Each buffer is typically 528 bytes, and can store the contents of one disk sector. The value for x depends on the amount of RAM memory available and the version of DOS. For a 640K machine running DOS 3.3 or 4, a value of x in the range 20 to 30 is usually appropriate.

FILES=*n* e.g. FILES=22

Many applications need to be able to open a number of files simultaneously. Database applications are particularly greedy in this respect. Set *n* equal to at least 20 if you run dBASE.

LASTDRIVE=[*letter*] e.g. LASTDRIVE=Z

If you intend to use the **subst** command to set up a virtual drive letter in place of a path, you will probably need to set LASTDRIVE to a letter lower down the alphabet than E which is the default setting. The usual thing to do is to include the statement LASTDRIVE=Z in the config.sys file.

DEVICE=[*drive:*] [\path\driver]

e.g. DEVICE=C:\SYS\MOUSE.SYS

Peripherals such as keyboards, video displays, printers, mice and so on need interface programs called device drivers which tell the computer system how the device should work.
Typical drivers include:

ANSI.SYS
PRINTER.SYS
MOUSE.SYS
VDISK.SYS
RAMDRIVE.SYS
KEYBOARD.SYS
COUNTRY.SYS

Installing device drivers

A neat way to do this is to make a subdirectory called SYS and collect together any files with the ending .SYS by copying them into the subdirectory. Certain .sys files originate from the version of DOS supplied with your machine, but devices such as a mouse or a network card will have special device drivers supplied with them.
If you install all your drivers into a directory such as \SYS, you must ensure that the operating system and other programs can find them by including statements such as DEVICE=C:\SYS\MOUSE.SYS in the config.sys file and also including the \SYS directory in the path command of your autoexec.bat file (*see* Task 26).

What the different device drivers do

ANSI.SYS controls the screen and the way in which graphics and colour are handled. Many programs will not run unless they have access to this driver.
PRINTER.SYS enables foreign language character sets to be printed on a printer that supports them.
MOUSE.SYS provides the interface driver for a mouse pointing device which is required by 'front-end' programs like WINDOWS.
VDISK.SYS and RAMDRIVE.SYS enable RAM memory to be used as a virtual disk drive. Such disks are known as **ramdisks** or **silicon disks**. They operate much faster than their magnetic counterparts and judicious use of them can speed up the

operation of applications which read and write to disks intensively. The trade off is that they tie up a substantial chunk of RAM memory, so you must be careful to leave sufficient RAM to run the application in the first place!

Warning! Data held in RAM disks will be lost when power is removed, so you should copy data to a real disk at regular intervals of ten or fifteen minutes.

If you have an AT with 1 Mbyte of RAM, programs can normally address only the first 640K of memory. You might as well use some of the additional memory as a RAM disk by placing the following statement into the CONFIG.SYS file:

```
device=c:\sys\vdisk.sys 256 128 128 /e
```

The first number specifies the disk size in Kilobytes, the default is 64K, the example above is 256K. The second number specifies the sector size in bytes; the default is 128. The third number specifies the number of files that can exist in the root directory of the virtual drive. The default is 64 and the maximum is 1024.

The /e switch is important as it tells DOS to use the spare memory above the 640K level. If you do not put this in, the virtual drive will steal memory from your applications. When you next boot up the computer, if you have installed the RAMDISK driver correctly you will get a message telling you the letter that has been assigned to your virtual disk:

```
VDISK Version 3.3 virtual disk D:
    Directory entries adjusted
    Transfer size adjusted
    Buffer size:      256 KB
    Sector size:      128
    Directory entries:64
    Transfer size:      8
```

From DOS v3.3 onwards, international character sets are stored in what are called code-pages. The keyboard and country device drivers enable the keyboard configuration and display the appropriate character set and date format.

For DOS 3.3 onwards you need to include the following statement in the config.sys file:

```
COUNTRY=44,,\SYS\COUNTRY.SYS
```

The ending ,\ SYS\COUNTRY.SYS is necessary only if you have collected all the .sys files into a subdirectory called \ SYS.

```
SHELL=[drive:] [\path\filename] /p /e:size
```

Warning! This statement is only necessary if you have DOS v3.2 or earlier. You can use it with the /e switch to set up a larger environment space.

Be careful with this statement because you can lock yourself out of the machine. **Always** have a floppy boot disk handy in case you inadvertently prevent the machine from booting from the hard disk. You can then re-boot from the floppy and return the hard disk to normal.

Notice that there are two switches. The /p switch tells DOS to keep the command processor permanently resident in memory. If this is omitted, command.com will allow itself to be displaced by other program instructions until the computer 'hangs up'.

For versions of DOS up to v3.2 *size* is the number of 16 byte chunks you want to set aside for environment variables. From DOS v3.2 onwards the number is expressed in actual bytes.

e.g.   `SHELL=C:\COMMAND.COM /E:16  /P`   [DOS v3.0]

`SHELL=C:\COMMAND.COM /E:256 /P`   [DOS v3.2]

Activity 25.1   Making your own CONFIG.SYS file and trying it out

It is advisable to experiment first before attempting to install your own config.sys file on a hard disk. For this exercise you will need the floppy boot disk that you created in Task 15. This was created by taking a new or unwanted disk, placing it in the floppy drive and typing:

`format a:/4/s` `ENTER`

Place your boot disk in drive A: and log onto it by typing

`A:` `ENTER`

You can construct a simple config.sys file by using a text editor or the **copy con** command you met in Task 8.

```
    cd \ ENTER
    copy con config.sys ENTER
buffers=20 ENTER
files=22 ENTER
country=44,,\sys\country.sys ENTER
device=\sys\ansi.sys ENTER
device=\sys\vdisk.sys 64 128 64 ENTER
Ctrl-z ENTER
```

Do not forget to hold down the `Ctrl` key and press `Z` to tell DOS you have reached the end of file.

If you reboot the computer now you will get error messages saying that the device drivers do not exist. You will install the device drivers in Activity 25.2.

If you discover that your system has the RAMdisk driver RAMDRIVE.SYS rather than VDISK.SYS you should include the line:

`device=\sys\ramdrive.sys 64 128 64`

instead of the one above which refers to vdisk.sys.

Activity 25.2   Installing the device drivers

Make a directory \SYS

        cd \ ENTER
        md sys ENTER

Then copy .SYS files from wherever they are located on your system. If you have a
hard disk you could try looking for them in the following most likely directories:

        \   (the root directory)
        \DOS
        \MS-DOS
        \SYS
        \BIN
        \UTILS

If the .sys files happen to be in the \ DOS directory, you would have to perform the
following steps:

        cd \dos ENTER
        copy *.sys a:\sys ENTER   (or b:\sys on a twin floppy drive machine)

Leave the system disk in drive A and reboot the computer by holding down the Ctrl
and Alt keys with two fingers of the left hand and pressing the Del key.

You should see the message telling you that the RAMDISK has been installed. To see
how memory has been affected, you could try running **chkdsk** on the virtual drive.

This is the output from chkdsk after installing RAMdisk. The computer had only 640K
of memory, so the extended memory switch /e was not used.

        C:\>chkdsk d: ENTER

        Volume VDISK V3.3 created Dec 6, 1984 12:00p

        256896 bytes total disk space
             0 bytes in 1 hidden files
        256896 bytes available on disk

        655360 bytes total memory
        332544 bytes free

Notice that by setting up a RAMdisk of 365k capacity only 332544 bytes of
memory remain. Applications software needing 512 Kbytes will now be unable to
run.

Reboot

When you have finished experimenting with your config file remove your practice system disk from the A drive and re-boot the computer in the normal way. If the config.sys file is either inadequate or does not exist you can now set up your own config.sys file. Keep it simple to start with:

```
buffers=20
files=20
device=c:\sys\ansi.sys
country=44,,c:\sys\country.sys
lastdrive=z
```

Key words	Config.sys

Task 26	**The autoexec.bat file**

Objective   To write a simple autoexec.bat file.

Instructions   When the computer boots up the command processor is loaded, the config.sys file is read and then DOS searches the root directory for a file called autoexec.bat. If this file is present it is automatically executed, hence its name.

Autoexec.bat is an example of a DOS batch file. A batch file in its simplest form is just a list of DOS commands which are executed one by one. You can include commands to set up the working environment of your computer. At its simplest an autoexec.bat file might contain the following lines, each line consisting of a DOS command:

```
C:\>type autoexec.bat ENTER

    echo off
    date
    time
    path=c:\;c:\dos;c:\sys;
    keybuk
    prompt $p$g
    pause
    cls
```

What each line means:

echo off
Unless the line echo off is included, each command will be echoed to the screen as it is executed; this can be confusing.

date, time
If the machine does not have a battery operated clock it is a good idea to force users to set the time and date so that files are date stamped accurately when they are created or updated.

path
The necessity for a **path** command was discussed in Task 12. A default path should be set up initially by the AUTOEXEC.BAT file. It can always be modified later.

keybuk (DOS 3.2 and earlier)
Keybuk is an external command that configures your keyboard so that it recognises keys such as the pound (£) sign. Together with the statement country=44 in the CONFIG.SYS file, **keybuk** establishes the English personality of your computer.

keyb (DOS 3.3 and later)
Keyb works together with the device driver KEYBOARD.SYS to establish a national identity. You must make the driver available to the **keyb** program, either by keeping them in the same directory, or by including the driver as an argument to the command.

See the example in Activity 26.1.

prompt e.g. Prompt pg
The prompt can be tailored to suit individual preferences. In the example above, I have
included the current path '$p' and the 'greater than' sign '$g'.

pause, cls
Before the screen is cleared by the command **cls**, the user has the opportunity to read
any system or error messages. The **pause** command temporarily suspends execution of
the program and invites the user to press any key to continue execution.

Activity 26.1   Writing the program

Place the boot disk that you were using in Task 25 into the A drive and log on.
Follow the steps:

```
a: ENTER
cd \ ENTER

copy con autoexec.bat ENTER
echo off ENTER
cls ENTER
path a:\sys ENTER
keyb uk,,\sys\keyboard.sys ENTER (or keybuk for DOS v3.2 and
                                                      earlier)
prompt $p$g ENTER
echo Welcome to the DOS operating system ENTER
date ENTER
```

Position the end-of-file marker by holding down the Ctrl key and pressing **z** then
press ENTER, or press F6 ENTER

Copy the **keyb** or **keybuk** command from your hard disk or systems disk to the
root directory of your practice disk. Check also that you have copied the .sys files to
the directory A:\sys.

Re-boot the system with Ctrl, Alt, Del and see how your autoexec file operates.

You should see the screen clear, then the welcome message will be displayed.
Before the prompt appears you will have the opportunity to reset the date.

Check that the path has been set correctly by typing:

```
set ENTER
```

When you have finished experimenting, remove your practice system disk from drive
A and re-boot the computer in the normal way. If there is no adequate
AUTOEXEC.BAT file in your system root directory, now is the time to create one.

You can move to the root directory and use **copy con** AUTOEXEC.BAT to create a simple autoexec file similar to the ones in the examples above.

When you have written and tested the program, protect both the AUTOEXEC.BAT file and the config.sys file from accidental erasure by using the **attrib** command (see Task 17).

```
attrib +r autoexec.bat ENTER
attrib +r config.sys ENTER
```

While you are doing this you could protect the .SYS files in the \ SYS directory.

```
cd \sys ENTER
attrib +r *.sys ENTER
```

Key words	Prompt
	Keyb
	Path
	Cls
	Pause

Section E: Programming in DOS ▬▬▬

In this final section you will learn how to write some simple but effective programs using the DOS commands you have already learned, together with some additional commands which are exclusive to batch processing.

Task 27

Filters, pipes and redirection

Objective

To use the filters **more**, **find** and **sort**.

Instructions

Filters

Before you get too involved in programming, there are some special commands called **filters** that you should know about. Filters tend to be used mostly within programs, but they can also be used as commands outside a program.

A filter command takes a stream of input data and performs an operation on it which produces a corresponding stream of output data.

The input data can come from a file, or it can be the output of another process. The output data is normally sent to the VDU screen, but it could equally well be sent to a file or to another process.

Pipelines

To enable the output of one command or process to become the input to a second command or process, we use the **pipe** symbol ' | ' to join the two processes.

Redirection

To enable the output of a command to be directed to a file or device other than the VDU, we use the redirection symbols > and >>. Input can be taken from a file by the reverse redirection sign <.

Activity 27.1

Using the **more** filter

This was covered briefly in Task 13. **More** filters output on its way to the VDU by splitting it up into screen pages with the message ---More--- at the bottom. This enables you to read a screen at a time, pressing a key to get the next page. In the example:

```
dir | more
```

The output of the **dir** command is connected by the **pipe** '|' to the input of the filter **more**. (Since you could type the command **dir /p**, you probably would not use **more** in that context.)

If you have a long file to display, or the output from a command such as **tree** is lengthy, you could filter it through **more**, e.g.

```
type longfile.doc | more ENTER
```

```
tree | more ENTER
```

Activity 27.2   The redirection symbols

Change to a directory with plenty of files in it so that there is a long listing when you type

```
dir ENTER
```

Redirect the directory listing into a file by typing:

```
dir > dir.lst ENTER
type dir.lst ENTER
```

You could stop the file from scrolling off the screen by piping the output of **type** into **more**:

```
type dir.lst | more ENTER
```

A rather more elegant practice (since it dispenses with the **type** command) is to redirect the contents of the file dir.lst into **more** by means of the reverse redirection symbol '<':

```
more < dir.lst ENTER
```

If your directory list was not long enough to scroll off the screen you could use the append redirection symbol to add another listing to the file:

```
dir >> dir.lst
```

If it is possible to use more < dir.lst, could you not also use the combination dir.lst << dir ? Try it (answer on p.122).

Activity 27.3   Using the **find** filter

Find searches the specified file to match the string of characters enclosed in quotation marks in the command line.

Syntax: `find "string" file`

e.g. `find "Pascal Ltd" phone.nos`

`---------- phone.nos`

`Pascal Ltd      071 346 7882`

Find takes its input from the file specified in the second argument of the command line and filters out the line(s) of the file which contain the string specified in the first argument.

In the example above the file phone.nos contains a list of names and telephone numbers. You can create such a file using copy con phone.nos — additional lines can be added by redirecting the output of the **echo** command to the file, e.g.

Create the file phone.nos containing a list of telephone numbers.

> `copy con phone.nos` `ENTER`

`Pascal Ltd`	`081 346 7882` `ENTER`	Type in these lines ending
`James Fryatt`	`0323 56657` `ENTER`	each with `ENTER`
`Passada Surfacing`	`081 455 6557` `ENTER`	
`Susan Short`	`071 334 4366` `ENTER`	
`Pascalite & Co`	`0223 11245` `ENTER`	
`Jasper Porritt`	`0986 32256` `ENTER`	
`Ctrl-Z` `ENTER`		

Additional lines can be added to the file by using the append redirection symbol '>>'. In the example below, the output of the **echo** command is redirected to the file phone.nos

> `echo Southern Building Society 03325 55457 >>phone.nos`

Now use the **find** filter to look up some numbers:

> `find "Pas" phone.nos` `ENTER`
> `find "Short" phone.nos` `ENTER`
> `find "071" phone.nos` `ENTER`

Activity 27.4   Connecting **dir** to **find**

You can pipe the output of a command such as **dir** into **find**. Here is a useful example; display only those files updated on a certain date, e.g.

```
dir | find "20-05-90" ENTER
```

You will have to choose a date appropriate to files in your directories.

Activity 27.5   The **sort** filter

Sort takes data directly from a file or piped from another command and produces sorted output which can be displayed on screen, redirected to another file or piped to another filter.

Syntax: `[Source command] | sort [switches]`
or
`sort [switches] <sourcefile`

Sort uses two switches:

/r   reverse sort, i.e. Z →A, 9–0
+n   where *n* is the number of the column to be sorted. If *n* is not specified, the file is sorted from the first character of the first column.

Try it on your phone.nos file:

```
sort    <phone.nos ENTER
echo    Annabel's 081 443 5647 >> phone.nos ENTER
type    phone.nos ENTER
type    phone.nos | sort ENTER
```

Sort produces only a sorted display. If you want the file itself to be sorted you should redirect the output to another file. Because **sort** creates a temporary work-file, it is possible to redirect the output back to the source file:

```
sort <phone.nos >phone.nos ENTER
type phone.nos
```

Where a file is consistently formatted into a series of columns, you can sort on a particular column. Try sorting the output of the **dir** command on the date column:

```
dir | sort +24 ENTER
```
(The date field is the 24th column)

Activity 27.6   Using the commands together

In this final exercise you can link all the **filter** commands together by pipes and redirection. Find a directory with a really long list of files in it, then display the directory listing of files date stamped 1990 one page at a time sorted on file size starting with the largest. Try to work it out for yourself first! (Answer on p.122.) Remember that **pipes** connect the output of a command to a **filter**; **redirection** connects output of a command to a file or device.

Key words   **More**
Find
Sort

Task 28　　Batch files – replaceable parameters

Objective　To write command files that use **replaceable parameters**.

Instructions　You have already written a number of very short batch programs consisting of standard DOS commands. A powerful feature of batch programming involves the use of variables called **replaceable parameters**.

You can continue to use **copy con** to create small example programs, but for longer and more complex ones it is recommended that you use an editor such as Norton Editor, Steed or even a word processing package as long as your program file is unformatted. For instance if using WordStar you must first open the file using N for Non-document mode.

General rules about batch programs　Batch programs must have a name made up of legal filename characters (see p.ix) and must end with the extension .BAT.

The name must not be the same as an existing DOS command or other executable program with the extension .COM .EXE or .BAT.

Batch files are executed by typing the filename only, not the extension.

Execution of a batch program can be interrupted by pressing `Ctrl–C`. The message `Terminate batch job (Y/N)?` is displayed.

Activity 28.1　Using a replaceable parameter

In Activity 27.3 you used the **find** command to search a file for a string entered in quotes, e.g.

```
find "Short" phone.nos ENTER or
find "Pascalite" phone.nos ENTER
```

You could make this query more efficient by a very simple batch file:

```
copy con phone.bat ENTER
find "%1" phone.nos ENTER
Ctrl-Z ENTER
```

To run the program, type

```
phone
```

followed by the string you are looking for, e.g.

```
phone Susan ENTER
----------phone.nos
Susan Short    071 334 4336
```

The string 'Susan' is substituted for the parameter %1 in the program. We used the first parameter out of a possible ten, hence the parameter name '%1'.

Try the command again:

```
phone Pas ENTER
phone Porritt ENTER
```

Now write a command to display a sorted list of files with a particular date stamp:

```
copy con files.bat ENTER
dir ¦ find "%1" ¦ sort /+24 ENTER
Ctrl-Z ENTER
```

To display a sorted list of files updated during 1990 type:

```
files -90 ENTER
```

For files updated in May 1990, type:

```
files 05-90 ENTER
```

Activity 28.2   Using more parameters

Suppose you wish to extract all the lines in the file PHONE.NOS that share a common feature, such as the prefix 071, and copy them to a file whose name you specify:

```
copy con extract.bat ENTER
find "%1" > %2.nos ENTER
Ctrl-Z ENTER
```

Now test out the command by typing:

```
extract 071 london ENTER
type london.nos ENTER
```

The command **extract** finds all the numbers with 071 and copies them to the file london.nos, because the second word 'london' on the command line replaced the second parameter %2 in the command.

Activity 28.3   Named parameters

In Tasks 12 and 24 you used the **set** command to assign values to variables in the DOS environment space. These variables can be accessed in batch file progams where they are called **named parameters**.

For instance to move a group of files from the root directory to a user directory, first set the environment variable to the user-name **USERC1**

    set user=USERC1 `ENTER`   (Environment variables are case sensitive)

    copy con move.bat `ENTER`
    cd \ `ENTER`
    md %user% `ENTER`
    copy *.%1 \ %user% `ENTER`
    del *.%1 `ENTER`
    `Ctrl-z` `ENTER`

Explanation

After making sure that you are in the root directory, the program makes a subdirectory whose name is whatever is currently stored in the variable **user**. Notice that the named parameter is enclosed within a pair of percentage signs. The current setting of %user% is USERC1, so a directory called USERC1 is made.

The next step is that files matching the extension equivalent to the first command line parameter are copied to the user area.

Finally the source files are deleted from the root directory.

If you typed the command: move mem `ENTER`

the line in the program: copy *.%1\%user%

would become: copy *.mem \userc1

Key words   **Find**
                       Extract
                       Set

Task 29　　　**Batch files – special commands**

Objective　　　To become familiar with the batch file processing commands **if**, **goto** and **for**.

Instructions　　　There are a number of special commands that can be used only within a DOS program. The commands are all internal, i.e. they are loaded into memory along with the command processor at boot-up.

　　　The special commands are: **call** (v3.3 and later), **echo off/on**, **for. .in. .do**, **goto**, **if**, **pause**, **rem**, **shift**

Activity 29.1　　　Program control using **if** and **goto**

Many batch programs expect to find data on the command line which will be substituted into a replaceable parameter. For instance, in the program on p.103 called phone.bat you ran the program by typing:

　　　phone Pascal `ENTER`

What happens if you type phone with no argument?　phone `ENTER`

Since you are not supplying a string for **find** to look for, there is no output from the program.

Consider this flow-chart:

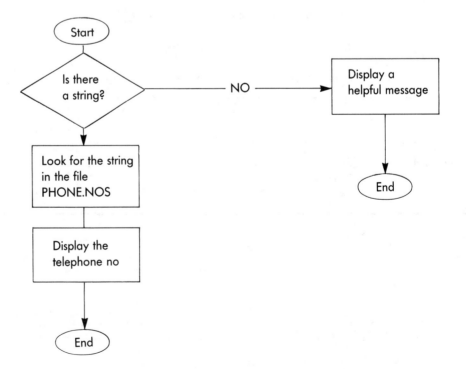

You could summarise the flowchart simply:

IF   there is a string on the command line:

        find the string in the file phone.nos
        display the name and telephone number
        end.

ELSE display the following message:

        you forgot to include the name after the command PHONE
        e.g.   PHONE LIZ

        end

This could be implemented as a DOS program as follows:

Program statements	Explanation
`echo off`	Prevents every line from being echoed
`cls`	Clears the screen
`if $%1==$ goto message`	If there is no string, goto :message (See more detailed explanation below)

`echo The number you require is:`
`find "%1" phone.nos`
`goto end`
	Skip over the error message

`:message`	Here is the labelled line to goto

`echo You forgot to include the name after`
`echo the command PHONE`
`echo e.g.         PHONE LIZ`	

`:end` `echo Thankyou for using the PHONE utility`	

Type in the program, leaving out the explanations on the right of the page.

Test it by running the program with and without a command line string.

The if syntax   There are three ways in which the **if** command can be used.

1 IF [not] *string1*==*string2* COMMAND

e.g. (a) `if $%1==$ GOTO message`

Here the string '$' plus whatever is contained in the first parameter %1, is tested against '$'. If the %1 parameter is empty, then $==$ and the condition is satisfied.

e.g. (b) IF %2==%user% ECHO Welcome %user%

In this example the test is to see if the second parameter %2 is equal to the data stored in the environment variable %user%.

e.g. (c) IF not %1==Netmgr CALL security

If the first parameter string %1 is not equal to 'Netmgr', the program called security is executed.

2 IF errorlevel *number* COMMAND

Certain commands return an **exit code** when they terminate. The numeric value of the exit code relates to the success or failure of the program. If the command executes successfully the code 0 is often returned,
e.g. IF not errorlevel 0 goto message

3   IF exist *filename* COMMAND

This is a useful variant of the **if** statement. A certain action can be performed *only* if a file exists.

e.g. IF exist accounts.tmp ren accounts.tmp accounts.dat

If the file accounts.tmp exists, rename it to accounts.dat

Activity 29.2   Testing the examples

Example 1(b) if %1==%user% COMMAND

First assign a name to the variable user:

   set user=Jenny `ENTER`

   copy con test.bat `ENTER`
   if %1==%user% echo Hi there %user% `ENTER`
   `Ctrl–Z` `ENTER`

   test Jenny `ENTER`

   test Ali `ENTER`

Example 1(c) `if not %1=="Netmgr" COMMAND`

```
copy con test.bat ENTER
if not %1=="Netmgr" echo You're not the Network Manager.
ENTER

Ctrl-Z ENTER

test anyone ENTER
test Netmgr ENTER
```

Example 3 `if exist filename command`

Create some temporary files `stock.tmp` and `order.tmp`:

```
echo example file1>stock.tmp ENTER
echo example file2 > order.tmp ENTER

copy con test.bat ENTER
if not exist %1.tmp goto end ENTER
ren %1.tmp %1.new ENTER
end:
Ctrl-Z ENTER

test stock ENTER
test order ENTER
test sales ENTER
```

Activity 29.3 The **for. . .in. . .do** construction

If you need to perform a command on a group of files that cannot be identified by a wild character or mask, it is sometimes possible to achieve this by using the **for in do** statement.

The general syntax is:

```
for %%c in (set of files) do command
```

e.g.   `for %%c in (*.prg *.ndx *.dbf) do copy %%c a:`

The command sets the variable %%c to each file in the set. In the example the set is all the dBASE program files, index files and database files. Each file in turn is copied to drive A.

Using the original practice disk in drive B, make a subdirectory called \ bak

Using the original practice disk in drive B, make a subdirectory called \ bak

```
b: ENTER
md bak ENTER

copy con test.bat ENTER
for %%c in (*.doc *.txt *.mem) do copy %%c \bak ENTER
Ctrl—Z ENTER

test ENTER
```

Key words	If
	Goto
	For. . .in. . .do

Batch files – electronic mail

To write programs to set up a simple menu system and an electronic mailbox.

Activity 30.1

Programming a menu driven 'front end'

When the computer boots up, it is often helpful for users to see a menu listing the options available, e.g.:

```
SOFTWARE MENU

1      Wordprocessing

2      Spreadsheet

3      Accounts system

4      Electronic Mail

5      MS-DOS commands

Please enter the number of your choice . . .
```

The menu system consists of a number of programs and files collected in a subdirectory which could be called \menu.

Program or file	comments
menu.bat	The main menu program
menu.txt	The text of the menu
1.bat	The program that enables the first choice from the main menu
2.bat	The second choice
n.bat	Further choice(s)

Program specifications:

A program specification can be a simple list of the main tasks that the program is supposed to achieve. The specifications can then be translated by the programmer into the computer language that is to be used, in this case the MS DOS command language.

Program specification for **menu.bat**

disable echoing of commands
clear the screen
display the text of the menu

General specification for the programs *1.bat, 2.bat,...,n.bat*

> disable echoing of commands
> clear the screen
> set a path to where the software is located
> call the application program
> after the application has finished ...
> return the user to the main menu

How to set up the menu system:

1 The menu text

First write the text file that displays the option menu. If you use a word processor for this task, make sure that the file is unformatted.

You could use the example in the box above, or you can make up your own menu. If you have a particular word processor, spreadsheet or other applications package, you could substitute its name for the more general options in the example menu.

2 The main menu program

You should be able to write the simple menu.bat program from the very explicit specification above! Try it for yourself.

3 The numbered batch files

Each choice is enabled by typing the number associated with that option. This means that for every choice there will be a batch file called *n*.bat, where *n* equals the option number.

Suppose:
> the first choice on the menu was WordStar;
> the WordStar program files live in a directory called **\ws**; and the document files are in a directory called **\user1doc**;
> ... then the program 1.bat might look like this:

```
                              *** comments ***
echo off
cls
set oldpath=%path%        * save the existing path
path= \ws                 * set the path to the software
append \ws                * enable DOS to find overlay files
cd\user1doc               * change to directory \ user1doc
ws                        * run WordStar
set path=%oldpath%        * set path to normal
cd\menu                   * change to menu directory
menu                      * run main menu program
```

A simpler version of the program might have dispensed with all the path commands, e.g:

```
echo off
cls
cd\ws
ws
cd\menu
menu
```

The disadvantage of the second example is that all the document files end up in the same directory as the program files. From the first example you can see that it is possible to allocate different users their own directories such as **\user1doc**.

Activity 30.2   Designing your own version of 2.bat

Design a batch file program with the name 2.bat that makes the following assumptions:

the program 2.bat will run the Lotus 123 spreadsheet;
the program files and overlays are in a directory called **\123**;
you run Lotus by the command '123';
the user files are located in the directory **\user3wks**;
the menu files are in the directory **\menu** as before.

Do not try to re-invent the wheel; follow the WordStar example closely. Do not type the program at this stage; in any case you may not even have Lotus 123 on your computer.

Once you understand how the idea works for one batch file of this type, you can quickly adapt the program to run another application.

Do not forget to allocate and create the appropriate user directories before you write the batch programs.

An electronic mail system   This project involves the use of the **if** command together with labels within the program to determine which options are executed.

You will now implement a command called **mail** that accepts command line arguments as follows:

mail *username* enables a message to be sent to the user specified by *username* `maid d` deletes the contents of the user's mailbox

`mail p` prints the contents of the user's mailbox

`mail s [file]` saves the user's mailbox to a file specified by `[file]`

`mail l` lists the current mailbox files

`mail h` displays a message reminding users what options are available and how to log on as mail users.

NB If no letter follows the contents of the user's mailbox will be displayed.

Before you can operate the electronic mail system you first log in to the mail box system. The specification for the login program is as follows:

```
program: login.bat

set echo off and clear screen
set environment variable to the current username
inform the user if there is mail to be read
display software menu
```

Activity 30.3	Programming the login command

The login program can implemented as follows:

```
copy con login.bat ENTER    * or use your text editor
set echo off ENTER
cls ENTER
set user=%1 ENTER            * sets the variable user to the value contained
                               in the parameter %1
if exist %user%.msg echo
pause
cd \menu ENTER
menu ENTER
Ctrl-Z ENTER
```

If you have not written the menu system in Activities 30.1 and 30.2 you will have to leave out the two lines containing the word 'menu'. When you run the program, you should type:

```
login username ENTER
```

e.g.
```
login Mandy ENTER
```

This will cause the username 'Mandy' to be stored in the environment variable user.

| **Activity 30.4** | Improving the login program |

If you attempt to log in to the mail system by typing the command **login** without including your *username* as a command line argument, the command will not be allowed to continue and a helpful error message will be displayed. By studying Activity 29.1 in the previous task, try to work out how you could improve the LOGIN.BAT program so that it traps an incorrect login attempt of this kind.

Specification for the mail program

The program will begin with a series of tests using the **if** statement to see which of the command line options has been chosen.

Depending on the option, the flow of the program will be directed to the label that precedes the program statements that will perform the required option.

The program could be specified in normal English something like this:

```
disable echo and clear the screen
if parameter 1 is "d"          goto label :delete
if parameter 1 is "p"          goto label :print
if parameter 1 is "1"          goto label : list
if parameter 1 is "h"          goto label :help
if parameter 1 is "s"          goto label :save
if parameter 1 is empty        goto label :display

:mail
type in the message
add it to the file called username.msg
end

:delete
display message "deleting user's mailbox"
delete the file user.msg
end

:save
copy user's mailbox file
     to the file specified in parameter 2

:print
print the user's mailbox file
end

:list
list the current users by displaying a directory listing of all
     files ending .msg
end

:help
type the text file mail.hlp which contains instructions on how to
     log in and use the mail program
end
```

115

```
:save
copy the user's mailbox file to the file specified in parameter %2
end

:display
type the current user's mailbox to the screen
end
```

Activity 30.5   Implementing the program skeleton

The basic skeleton of the program consists of the tests, labels, and one echo
statement. You will need to use your editor to write, amend and de-bug your
program. In view of this, the copy con command should be dispensed with, except
within the program itself, where it will be used for writing the mail message.

Start off by typing in the following lines into your program which should be called
MAIL.BAT

```
rem mail.bat
echo off
cls

if $%1==$ goto display
if %1==d  goto delete

:display
echo **** This is %user%'s current mailbox ****
goto end

:delete
echo **** Deleting %user%'s current mailbox ****
goto end

:end
echo Finished mailing
```

Testing both the   When you have typed in the program, test it by typing
programs login
and mail
```
login fred ENTER
mail ENTER
```

The computer should respond:

```
    **** This is fred's current mailbox ****
Finished mailing
```

If you type:

```
mail d ENTER
```

the computer should respond:

```
**** Deleting fred's current mailbox ****
Finished mailing
```

Activity 30.6   Adding more options

Add tests for the options p (print), h (help) s (save) and l (list). Do not forget; you are only creating the bare bones of the program; after the label you should include an appropriate echo statement only. It does not matter in what order the labels appear except that the label **:end** must be the last one.

Test the program by typing the command followed by the options **p**, **h**, **s** and **l**

```
mail p ENTER
mail h ENTER
mail l ENTER
mail s ENTER
```

If you did this correctly, the message that matches that option should be displayed, e.g.:

```
mail s fred.ml
Saving fred's mailbox to file : fred.ml
```

This assumes that you included these lines in your skeleton.

```
: save
2 echo saving %user%'s mailbox to file : %2
```

Activity 30.7   Putting flesh on the bones

The skeleton program tests for the command line options **d, s p, h** and **l**. It also deals with the case where there is no command line option. If you type a *username* on the command line, then all of the tests above will fail and the line immediately after the **if** statements will be executed.

We therefore place the statements that enable the sending of a mail message immediately after the tests so that these lines are executed by default if the tests fail.

Using your text editor, insert the following lines immediately after the last **if** statement:

```
:mail
echo type in your message to %1 now
echo (end your message file by typing Ctrl-Z
copy con mail.tmp
copy %1.msg + mail.tmp mail.tmp
echo **************************>>%1.msg
del mail.tmp
goto end
```

Note that you type the message into a temporary file called MAIL.TMP. This file is then added to the existing mail file using the copy command. A row of asterisks is appended to the end of the file in order to separate one message from the next. Finally the temporary file is deleted.

The completed MAIL.BAT program file is on pages 123–4 for you to refer to if necessary.

You have covered all the programming tricks needed to convert the remaining parts of the specification on **p** to actual DOS program statements. Try to implement them yourself if possible. When you have finished this project you will be able to write useful DOS programs for yourself and others.

Key words	cd
	login
	Ctrl–z
	if
	mail

Appendix

Solutions to exercises

Task 4
Activity 2

Prompt $L sets the prompt to the 'Less Than' sign: '<'

Prompt $ means no string of characters, so the prompt vanishes. You could type **prompt $** followed by **CLS** to clear the screen. A completely empty screen with no prompt at all looks quite eerie! It is even worse if you switch the cursor off as well, as you will discover yourself...

Task 4
Activity 8

Setting up the Purchasers branch of the tree
Purchasers is too long for a directory name, so why not call it BUYERS?

Follow these clues

1   Change Directory to the root (\ )
2   Make Directory BUYERS
3   Change Directory to BUYERS
4   Make Directories LOWPRICE, MIDPRICE and TOPPRICE
5   Change Directory to LOWPRICE
6   MAKE Directories A-D, E-K etc

Task 5
Activity 3

Investigating other drives
If you have a hard disk, change to drive C by typing:

C : `ENTER`

If not, insert a different disk in the floppy drive.
Look for files with extensions .DOC

Task 10
Activity 1

```
cd \  ENTER
```

```
COPY *.BAT \PROPERTY \DETACHED  ENTER
```

Task 10
Activity 1
(cont'd)

Step 1

```
cd \PROPERTY \DETACHED  ENTER
```

Step 2

```
dir *.*  ENTER
```

Step 3

```
del *.*  ENTER
```

Task 10
Activity 3

Removing the remaining subdirectories

cd \PROPERTY `ENTER`   (move to the parent directory)

dir *. `ENTER`   (list the directories)

RD FLATS `ENTER`

If this did not work because FLATS was not empty, you will have to go in and delete the files there:

CD FLATS `ENTER`

DIR *.* `ENTER`   (check that these are files you want to delete)

DEL *.* `ENTER`

CD .. `ENTER`   (drop back to the parent directory)

RD FLATS `ENTER`

Task 10
Activity 4

Removing the subdirectory PROPERTY

cd \PROPERTY `ENTER`

dir *.* `ENTER`

del *.* `ENTER`

cd .. `ENTER` (change to the root directory, which is the parent of PROPERTY)

rd PROPERTY `ENTER`

dir *. PROPERTY `ENTER`   (hopefully it should have gone!)

Task 11
Activity 1

Setting up the practice directory

md Task11 `ENTER` [Make Directory]

cd Task11 `ENTER` (Change Directory)

copy \ *.* `ENTER`[copy **all** files from the root]

Task 11
Activity 2

copy *.WKS *.WK2 `ENTER`
dir *.WK? `ENTER`

copy *.MEM *.MSG `ENTER`
dir *.M?? `ENTER`

Task 11 **Activity 5**	**1** `ren *.DAT *.BAK` `ENTER` **2** `copy SALARY.FEB SALARY.MAY` `ENTER` **3** `ren SALARY.FEB SALARY.MAY` `ENTER` This should produce a duplicate file error, because you had already created a file in **2** called SALARY.MAY

Task 13
Tree
	Activity 1: Here is the complete sequence of commands to make directories below the three you made at the start of the activity:
	
	`cd user` `ENTER` [change to USER which will be the parent of JOE and SUE]
	
	`md joe` `ENTER` [to make a directory, type MD space, followed by the name of the
	`md sue` `ENTER` directory you want to make]
	
	`cd \ data` `ENTER` [you must include the oblique '\' because DATA is a branch of
	root]
	
	`md memo` `ENTER`
	`md docs` `ENTER`
	`md accounts` `ENTER`

Task 13
Activity 3
	Copying files into the new directory structure
	
	`cd \` `ENTER`
	
	`copy *.EXE \SYSTEM` `ENTER`
	`copy *.COM \SYSTEM` `ENTER`
	
	`copy *.DAT \DATA` `ENTER`
	
	`copy *.DOC \DATA\DOCS` `ENTER`
	`copy *.TXT \DATA\DOCS` `ENTER`
	
	`copy admin*.* \DATA\ACCOUNTS` `ENTER`
	`copy ACC*.* \DATA\ACCOUNTS` `ENTER`
	
	`copy *.MEM\DATA\MEMO` `ENTER`

Task 17 **Activity 2**	If you protect all files with the command **attrib +r *.*** you will deny yourself access to those files which legitimately need updating. The general rule is that program and system files having names ending in .com .exe .ovl .bat. and .sys should be protected.
Task 27 **Activity 2**	If you tried the combination dir.lst << dir you would get the error message **Bad command or filename**, because the first word of the combination is not a command. You can use reverse redirection into a filter, e.g: **more < dir.lst**. Here **more**, which is a command, is taking its input from the file **dir.lst**.

Task 27
Activity 6

You must be careful of the order in which the commands are piped together:

```
dir ¦ find '-90' ¦ sort /+14/r ¦ more ENTER
```

Task 29
Activity 1

The menu program:

```
copy con menu.bat ENTER
```

```
set echo off ENTER
cls ENTER
type menu.txt ENTER
Ctrl-z ENTER
```

Activity 2 Design of the batch file 2.bat

```
echo off
cls
set oldpath=%path%
set path \123
append \123
cd \user3wks
123
set path=%oldpath%
cd \menu
menu
```

Task 30
Activity 1

```
echo off
cls
if $%1==$ goto help
set user=%1
if exist %user%.msg echo There is mail
pause

cd \menu
menu
goto end

:help
echo you must include your username after the command login
echo e.g.: login emma
```

Task 30
Activity 6

```
rem mail.bat
echo off
cls

if $%1==$       goto display
if %1==d        goto delete
if %1==p        goto print
if %1==h        goto help
if %1==l        goto list
if %1==s        goto save
```

```
:display
echo **** This is %user%'s current mailbox ****
goto end

:delete
echo **** Deleting %user%'s current mailbox ****
goto end

:print
echo **** Printing %user%'s current mailbox ****
goto end

:help
echo **** How to use the MAIL program ****
goto end

:list
echo **** List of current users ****
goto end

:save
echo **** Saving %user%,s current mailbox file to %2

:end
echo finished mailing
```

The complete program file mail.bat

```
@echo off            * leave out the @ sign in DOS v3.2 and earlier

cls

if $%1==$ goto display
if %1==d  goto delete
if %1==p  goto print
if %1==h  goto help
if %1==l  goto list
if %1==s  goto save

:mail
echo type in your message to %1
echo end the message file by typing ctrl-z
copy con mail.tmp
echo Message from %user% >>%1.msg
copy %1.msg + mail.tmp %1.msg
echo *************************>>1.msg
del mail.tmp
goto end

:display
echo **** This is %user%'s current mailbox ****
type c:\mail\%user%.msg
goto end
```

```
:delete
echo **** Deleting %user%'s current mailbox ****
echo Press ctrl-c to abandon this operation
pause
del c:\mail\%user%.msg
goto end

:print
echo **** Printing %user%'s current mailbox ****
echo Please make sure printer is ready . . .
pause
type c:\mail\%user%.msg >prn
goto end

:help
echo **** How to use the MAIL program ****
type c:\mail\mail.hlp
goto end

:list
echo **** List of current users' mail box files ****
dir c:\mail\*.msg
goto end

:save
echo **** Saving %user%'s current mailbox file to %2
copy %user%.msg %2

:end
echo Finished mailing
```

Whatever software package you are learning...

- dBase III+ ● Sage Book-keeper ● Multiplan
- Lotus 1-2-3 ● Ventura ● DataEase ● Pegasus
- SmartWare

You will find a book in the Pitman *Training Guide* series suited to your needs.

Ask for the titles in the *Training Guide* series in your local bookstore.
Alternatively, contact our sales department:
Pitman Publishing, 128 Long Acre, London WC2E 9AN
Telephone: 071-379 7383